Richard Dawkins Lies Like a Rug

Douglas Sczygelski

Published by Douglas Sczygelski, 2018.

While every precaution has been taken in the preparation of this book, the publisher assumes no responsibility for errors or omissions, or for damages resulting from the use of the information contained herein.

RICHARD DAWKINS LIES LIKE A RUG

First edition. August 28, 2018.

Copyright © 2018 Douglas Sczygelski.

ISBN: 979-8230602552

Written by Douglas Sczygelski.

Table of Contents

To my family, from whom I learned so much.

RICHARD DAWKINS
LIES LIKE A RUG

All the information in this e-book can be found in the chapter about Richard Dawkins in the book *Darwin Wanted to Exterminate the Blacks, and Other Facts about Famous Atheists*, by the same author.

Introduction

Richard Dawkins, a British biologist, became famous by writing books about evolution. Perhaps he knows a great deal about biology. I'm really not qualified to say. But then he wrote a book about religion and morality called *The God Delusion*, which is so full of lies and faulty reasoning that one has to suspect that he knew perfectly well that it was full of lies and faulty reasoning, but just didn't care. All he cared about was making a pile of money by telling atheists what they wanted to hear, and he succeeded: the book sold well and the money rolled in.

Let me make a few comments.

Item 1: Hitler

On pages 272-278 of his book *The God Delusion*, (pages 308-315 of the paperback) Richard Dawkins argues that Hitler was not an atheist. His evidence is paltry. First, he points out that in *Mein Kampf* and in speeches now and then, Hitler said he believed in God. So what? Hitler lied constantly, as every historian knows. One should never assume he really meant what he said.

Second, Dawkins claims that in 1941, Hitler told General Gerhard Engel, "I shall remain a Catholic forever." His source for that quote is an article by some guy named Richard E. Smith in a magazine called *Freethought Today*. Dawkins says we can look up that article on the Internet at http://www.FFRF.org/FTToday/1997/march97/ holocaust, but when I tried to do that, all that showed up on the screen was a letter about Hitler that an atheist organization sent to President George W. Bush. The letter doesn't mention that statement that Dawkins says Smith says Hitler made to General Engel.

Why should we believe Richard E. Smith anyway? Is he a reputable history professor or journalist? Dawkins doesn't say. Believe it or not, Dawkins apparently assumes that anything printed in a magazine article must be true. Doesn't he know that it is pretty common for liars to make up phony quotes and attribute them to famous people? If he doesn't know that, he should try reading a book on this subject called *They Never Said It*, which was written by two college professors, Paul F. Boller, Jr. and John George, and published by the Oxford University Press, one of the most prestigious publishing houses in the world. Boller and George show that many famous quotes were never spoken by the famous people who allegedly said them. And what about that magazine *Freethought Today* that Dawkins says printed this alleged quote from Hitler? Does it have a good reputation for honesty, or is it run by crackpots? Apparently Dawkins never even thought of that question. I quote from magazine articles quite often, but only from high-quality magazines that have good reputations for accuracy.

Furthermore, the quote is implausible on its face. When, in his entire adult life, did Hitler ever attend services in a Catholic church? Never. When, in his entire adult life, did he ever go to confession, something which every Catholic is required to do at least once per year? Never. If he was a Catholic, why did he repeatedly go to bed with his girlfriend Eva Braun without marrying her first? Dawkins seems to have never thought of that question. Did any friend, employee or colleague ever report seeing Hitler reading the Bible or any other religious book? Neither Dawkins nor anyone else ever mentions any such incident. Did any of Hitler's friends or assistants ever report seeing him pray? Neither Dawkins nor anyone else mentions anything like that. Just look at the critically-acclaimed two-volume biography of Hitler that was written by a prominent history professor named Ian Kershaw. It says nothing about Hitler going to church or going to confession or having any kind of religious life. Surely Kershaw would've mentioned something about Hitler's religious life, if he had had one. The first volume of Kershaw's biography of Hitler was published in 1998 and the second volume in 2000, so Dawkins could have consulted them to get the facts about Hitler's life when he was writing *The God Delusion*, if he had wanted to. Obviously he didn't want to. Instead he wanted to get his information from people who would tell him the lies that he wanted to hear.

Isn't that amusing? On the subject of evolution, Dawkins says the skeptics are a bunch of crackpots and we should all believe what the college professors tell us. But when the question is whether Hitler was religious, he suddenly decides that college professors aren't a good source of information after all. Instead he believes what he reads in some obscure magazine.

And to top it all off, look at what John Cornwell says in his book *Hitler's Pope*. Cornwell spends the whole book throwing mud at Pope

Pius XII, very unfairly in my opinion, but even Cornwell admits, on page 116, that in 1930 the Vatican's official newspaper declared that Catholics were not allowed to belong to the Nazi Party. So if Hitler was a Catholic, as Dawkins claims, why did he not quit the Nazi Party in 1930? On pages 126 and 127 of *Hitler's Pope*, Cornwell admits that in 1932, the Catholic bishops of Germany issued a declaration repeating what the Vatican newspaper said in 1930, that Catholics were not allowed to belong to the Nazi Party. Once again, that did not cause Hitler to quit the Nazi Party. If he was a Catholic, as Dawkins claims, why did he not do that? Then on pages 146 and 147 of *Hitler's Pope*, Cornwell admits that in June 1933, a "rally of Catholic apprentices" in Munich drew 25,000 participants, but it was broken up by Nazi thugs who beat up the Catholic apprentices and chased them off the streets when they tried to hold a march and rally. If Hitler was a Catholic, as Dawkins claims, why did he let his followers do that?

Anyone can see what is going on here. Dawkins simply doesn't want his readers to know the truth. His goal is to spread lies.

Then, on page 274 of *The God Delusion*, (page 311 of the paperback) Dawkins says we should believe Hitler believed in God because a man named John Toland, who wrote a book about Hitler, said so. Why should we believe John Toland? Dawkins doesn't say. He doesn't mention any evidence that was cited by Toland to support this claim. He wants us to just take Toland's word on faith. How odd. Dawkins won't take anything Jesus said on faith, but apparently he thinks John Toland was infallible.

The truth is that Toland was not a history professor nor a reputable journalist. He was merely a guy who wrote books about history for a living. He was a good writer, he knew how to make history come alive on the page, so some of his books became bestsellers and he made a lot of money from his writing, but that is not the same thing as being a true historian. He is most notorious for making the accusation, in his book *Infamy*, that Franklin Roosevelt knew from intelligence sources that Japan was about to attack Pearl Harbor, but refused to warn the American commanders there because he wanted America to suffer a major surprise defeat that would make the American people angry enough to declare war on Japan and Germany. (Endnote 1.) To put it mildly, that is a theory that reputable historians do not believe (the *Los Angeles Times* called it "widely discredited") and I would be very surprised to hear that Dawkins believes it.

Of course, even though Toland was a crackpot conspiracy theorist, that doesn't mean he was wrong about everything, but it does mean that a sensible person isn't going to believe Toland without supporting evidence. Dawkins doesn't tell us what evidence led Toland to claim Hitler believed in God, so there is no way we can take the claim seriously. Apparently it never occurred to Dawkins that his readers might want to know what the evidence was. I looked through Toland's book about Hitler, and I didn't see any supporting evidence at all.

And that is all the evidence Dawkins presents before concluding that Hitler "probably" believed in God: statements from Hitler, who lied constantly, one article in an obscure magazine, and one unsupported statement from a crackpot conspiracy theorist who wrote popular history books. Apparently Dawkins thought his readers would be so gullible that they would be convinced by this rubbish.

Now let us look at some of the evidence that Dawkins doesn't mention. In addition to the evidence that I already mentioned, let us remember that Hitler was not a churchgoer, nor, as near as I can tell, were any of his top advisors and assistants. (If there was any evidence that they were, surely the militant atheists would talk about it frequently.) Three of Hitler's top assistants, Alfred Rosenberg, Heinrich Himmler, and Martin Bormann, openly said that they were anti-Christian. Bormann once publicly declared that "National Socialism and Christianity are irreconcilable." (Endnote 2.) Saul Friedlander, a history professor at UCLA and one of the world's leading experts on the Holocaust, has written that the Nazi party "elite" was "generally hostile to Christian beliefs." (Endnote 3.) Hitler himself once stated publicly that the Nazi Party was not a movement of "puritans," that he didn't care if Catholic priests violated their vows of celibacy with adult women. (Endnote 4.)

Saul Friedlander, the renowned history professor whom I just mentioned, quotes Hitler as saying, "The worst blow to have hit humankind is Christianity. Bolshevism is a bastard child of Christianity. Both are the monstrous products of the Jews." (Endnote 5.) How can this be reconciled with the claim in *Freethought Today* magazine that Hitler said in 1941 that he would remain a Catholic forever? I think the obvious explanation is that the quote from *Freethought Today* magazine is phony. No history professor who has written about Hitler has ever quoted it, as near as I can tell, which indicates that the history professors think it is a phony quote.

Look at what William Shirer has to say. Shirer was an American who worked for CBS Radio News and covered Europe during the 1930s and 1940s. After the war, he was fired by CBS, basically because his bosses thought he was too liberal. (Endnote 6.) In the 1950s, Shirer wrote a massive book called *The Rise and Fall of the Third Reich* that became an enormous bestseller and made him a rich man. On page 100 of that book, he writes that Friedrich Nietzsche, the famous German atheist philosopher who coined the phrase, "God is dead," was very influential in Nazi Germany. "Nazi scribblers never tired of extolling him," Shirer says. "Hitler often visited the Nietzsche museum in Weimar and publicized his veneration for the philosopher by posing for photographs of himself staring in rapture at busts of the great man."

Are there any photographs of Hitler "staring in rapture" at pictures or statues of Jesus? Not that I know of. I've never heard any atheist mention any. But there was no end to Hitler's admiration for this atheist philosopher Nietzsche who spent his life pouring scorn on Christianity. Dawkins never mentions that.

After the success of *The Rise and Fall of the Third Reich*, Shirer wrote a few more books. On pages 149-156 of his book, *Twentieth Century Journey: The Nightmare Years, 1930-1940*, he writes about the Nazi persecution of German Christians. He talked to quite a few of these victims himself before they were arrested, and was impressed by their courage. On page 153, for example, he writes about a rally of 20,000 Protestants that occurred near Berlin on November 8, 1934, to denounce Nazi plans to take over Protestant churches. One of the speakers said, "We are fighting against the defamation of Christ and true Christianity. There are false prophets abroad in this land preaching the doctrine of blood and soil and racial mysticism, which we reject." The famous clergyman Martin Niemoller said at the rally, "It is a question of which master the German Protestants are going to serve: Christ or another." But on page 156, Shirer concludes that "the vast majority" of Germans were simply not interested in the fact that thousands of German Christians, both Catholic and Protestant, had been sent to concentration camps. "Not many Germans lost much sleep over the arrests of a few thousand pastors, priests and nuns," he writes. Instead, they cared about the fact that Hitler had ended unemployment, was rebuilding the army and navy, and was making Germany respected again on the world stage.

Listen to that. Hitler arrested "thousands" of pastors, priests and nuns. When did he ever arrest anyone for being an atheist? I've never heard anyone claim that.

Militant atheists always seem to assume that the clergymen of Germany could have overthrown Hitler by ordering their followers out into the streets, the same way massive demonstrations overthrew the Shah of Iran in 1979. It isn't true. Plenty of people in Germany in those days were in the habit of going to church on Sunday, but that doesn't mean they were zealous enough to risk their lives. And of course, many of the churchgoers were women and elderly men. There was no way

Hitler was going to be overthrown by a crowd of women and elderly men. The idea is ludicrous.

One must also remember that Germans, in those days, seemed to seriously believe that patriotism and blind obedience to the government were the same thing. Anja Rosmus is a German lady who got into a world of trouble a few years ago because, when she was in high school, she tried to find out what happened in her home town during the Nazi years. She dug up a lot of facts that many people would've preferred to forget. Eventually a movie called *The Nasty Girl* was made, based on the story of her investigation and the hostile reaction that resulted from it. Among other things, she has said, "A priest was murdered for defending the Jews in church. Another priest refused to swear an oath of loyalty to Hitler. He was killed too. But nobody ever spoke about these men with any respect. They had broken the rules. They were disobedient." (Endnote 7.)

Dawkins also fails to mention that on June 30, 1934, when Hitler carried out his famous "Blood Purge," four of the victims, executed without a trial and without having committed any crime, were prominent Catholic laypeople: Erich Klausener, the head of Catholic Action, the main service organization of Catholic laypeople in Germany; Adalbert Probst, the leader of the Catholic sports association; Fritz Gerlich, former editor of the Catholic newspaper, *Der Gerade Weg*; and Fritz Beck, the leader of a Catholic college student association. (Endnote 8.) To add insult to injury, the Nazis cremated their bodies, which was forbidden by church law in those days. (Endnote 9.) The German bishops and the Vatican uttered not one peep of protest against these murders. Lewy concludes that they were simply afraid that if they started an all-out struggle against Hitler, the laypeople would not back them up, and they would be crushed. (Endnote 10.)

Now, if Hitler was a Catholic, as Dawkins claims, why did he murder these four prominent Catholic laypeople in cold blood and have them cremated? Dawkins never asks that question. He doesn't want his readers to think about it.

Next, there is the fact that on July 25, 1934, some Austrian Nazis assassinated the Austrian dictator, an old-fashioned Catholic named Engelbert Dollfuss. Nobody has ever proven that Hitler ordered the murder of Dollfuss, but no historian seriously doubts it either. It is undeniable that Hitler was glad when he heard the news. Someone who was with him at the time has written, "he could scarcely wipe the delight from his face." (Endnote 11.) Pope Pius XI, on the other hand, was depressed by the news. He believed democracy inevitably led to rule by demagogues like Hitler and Mussolini, so a Catholic dictator such as Dollfuss was exactly the kind of man he liked seeing in leadership positions. But he did not condemn Hitler for it, because he believed that would do more harm than good. (Endnote 12.)

If Hitler was a Catholic, as Dawkins claims, why did he kill Dollfuss? By no stretch of the imagination could Hitler have believed that the pope wanted Dollfuss killed.

Hitler also outlawed all Catholic lay organizations, such as the Catholic Young Men's Association. Instead, he made membership in the Hitler Youth compulsory, even though Hitler Youth meetings contained what the German Catholic bishops considered anti-Christian propaganda. The bishops complained many times, but always backed down in the end. Then Hitler outlawed all Catholic daily newspapers, and some of the Catholic weeklies too. The remaining Catholic weeklies had to submit to censorship. (Endnote 13.)

If Hitler was a Catholic, as Dawkins claims, why did he do those things?

Then in 1937, Pope Pius XI issued *Mit Brennender Sorge*, a pastoral letter to the German people, in which he complained about Hitler's persecution of the Catholic Church and denounced Nazi ideology. (You can read about *Mit Brennender Sorge* in Wikipedia, or in Guenter Lewy's book *The Catholic Church and Nazi Germany*, or in John

Cornwell's book *Hitler's Pope*, and you can read the whole text of it on the Internet.) Did Hitler obey the pope and mend his ways? Of course not. The pope's opinion meant nothing to him. Why does Dawkins fail to notice that?

Statistics about Nazi crimes in Poland do not exist for many times and places, but we know that in October and November 1939, the Nazis murdered 214 Polish Catholic priests. (Endnote 14.) We also know that between September 1, 1939, and October 1, 1941, seventy-four Polish Catholic priests were murdered by the Nazis in the archdiocese of Poznan alone. (Endnote 15.) In October 1941, a Polish Catholic bishop named Leon Wetmanski was killed in the Auschwitz concentration camp. (Endnote 16.)

If Hitler really was a Catholic, as Dawkins claims, why did he kill so many Catholic priests in Poland? Don't hold your breath waiting for Dawkins to answer that question, or even mention that it happened. He doesn't want his readers to think about it.

Then there is the fact that in April 1941, Adolf Wagner, a Nazi bigwig in Bavaria, a region in southern Germany, ordered all crucifixes removed from Bavarian schoolrooms. What followed was, by the standards of Nazi Germany, significant unrest. Many parents kept their children home from school, and petitions with thousands of signatures, demanding the restoration of the crucifixes, were sent to Hitler. Wagner eventually revoked his order. There were other incidents in which local Nazi officials tried to ban school prayer, or seized monastery buildings from the Church and used them for Nazi Party offices. (Endnote 17.)

If Hitler was a Catholic, as Dawkins claims, why did his regime do such things? The answer is obvious: Hitler was not a Catholic at any time in his adult life. When Dawkins says otherwise, he is ignoring the facts.

Even Dawkins's friend, Harvard psychology professor Steven Pinker, has admitted that the idea that Hitler was a Catholic during his adult life, or any kind of Christian, is not true. (Endnote 18.) So why did Dawkins make that false statement? Maybe it was just an honest mistake, but it is hard to see how a well-educated man such as Dawkins could have failed to see that if you want to know the facts about Hitler's life, you should read books about him written by respectable history professors, rather than relying on the crackpot sources of information that Dawkins relied on. The more likely explanation is that Dawkins knew perfectly well that he was lying when he said Hitler was a Catholic during his adult life, but just didn't care. He is an atheist, he has no fear of Hell, so he was willing to deceive his readers as long as he could make a few bucks in the process.

You see, Dawkins had a problem. If he admitted that Hitler and Stalin, the two biggest mass murderers in human history, were both atheists, that would've made it tough to argue that atheism is just as good as Christianity at producing good moral behavior. For his pro-atheism book to be a bestseller, he needed to tell the atheists what they wanted to hear, and they definitely would not enjoy hearing the truth. So he decided that the best way to handle the problem was to lie his way through it. He had to admit that Stalin was an atheist, because Stalin had often declared himself to be one, but Hitler never publicly said, bluntly, that he was an atheist, so Dawkins saw an opportunity to fool people in Hitler's case.

The simple fact is that the four biggest mass murderers of the twentieth century, Hitler, Stalin, Mao and Pol Pot, were all atheists. Lee Harvey Oswald and James Earl Ray were atheists too, and Timothy McVeigh was an agnostic. You can read about this in detail in my book *Christianity Has a Better Moral Record Than Atheism.*

Item 2: The Manx Shearwater

On page 87 of his book *The God Delusion* (page 112 of the paperback), Dawkins tells a weird story that makes him look like an idiot, though he doesn't seem to realize that. He claims that when he was in college, a friend of his went on a camping trip in Scotland. "In the middle of night," Dawkins writes, "he and his girlfriend were woken in their tent by the voice of the devil – Satan himself; there could be no possible doubt: the voice was in every sense diabolical." Dawkins goes on to say he was "impressed" by this story, and the friend became a clergyman, partly because of it. Years later, Dawkins heard about a bird called a Manx shearwater that makes spooky noises, and decided that was probably the source of the noise his friend heard.

First, I don't believe this story. If it really happened, why doesn't Dawkins tell us his friend's name? Second, if this story really happened, then Dawkins is an imbecile. Why in the world would he be "impressed" by this tale? If a friend of mine told me a story like that, I would imagine the source of the noise was probably some local goofball who knows how to make scary noises and who enjoys wandering around the woods at night, scaring campers. The last thing I would imagine is that Satan was doing it. A little kid might think Satan was doing it, but, let me repeat, Dawkins says he was in college when he heard this story and believed it. Was he really that stupid?

Item 3: Evil Things Done in the Name of Atheism

On page 278 of *The God Delusion*, (page 315 of the paperback) Dawkins says "Individual atheists may do evil things, but they don't do evil things in the name of atheism." He seems to think this is a major point, and that it proves something significant. The truth, of course, is that it is a trivial point. Why can't Dawkins see that? The important question is not whether evil things are done "in the name" of atheism, but whether atheism leads to worse behavior than Christianity does.

Of course, even so, Dawkins is wrong to say evil things aren't done in the name of atheism. Just to state one famous example, when the communist atheists in Hungary arrested Cardinal Mindszenty and tortured him into falsely confessing to various crimes, does Dawkins really believe the fact that they were atheists was not part of their motivation? If atheism didn't motivate the arrest of Cardinal Mindszenty, what did? Does Dawkins seriously believe the atheists who ran the Hungarian government arrested Mindszenty at random, not because he was the leader of the Catholic Church in Hungary?

The same can be said about all the communist and Nazi persecutions of religion in the twentieth century.

Also on page 278, (page 316 in the paperback) Dawkins says he can't think of any war that has been "fought in the name of atheism." Has he never heard of the Korean War? Why does he think the atheists who ruled North Korea invaded South Korea in 1950? Every historian will tell you they had several reasons, and one of them was the desire to destroy religion in South Korea, just as they had destroyed it in North Korea. One could say the same about China's invasion of Tibet, the Soviet invasion of Poland in 1939, the Soviet invasion of Lithuania, Latvia, and Estonia in 1940, and the revolt of the Khmer Rouges in

Cambodia that started in the 1960s and culminated in their victory in 1975.

Dawkins finds it easy to imagine that a religious person might want to use force to impose his or her beliefs on others, but finds it absolutely impossible to imagine that an atheist might want to do so. What process of logic could possibly have led him to such a strange conclusion? The most likely explanation is that he knows perfectly well that he is babbling nonsense, but just doesn't care.

Item 4: Dawkins Blames the Jews

On page 271 of *The God Delusion* (page 307 of the paperback) Dawkins claims that it is because of science, not the Bible, that we believe that black people are human. He says the idea that blacks are human is a "deeply unbiblical idea."

A more outrageous lie would be hard to imagine. Nothing in the Bible says that. Dawkins doesn't cite one single verse in the Bible that says that, because he can't. There are none. In fact, chapter 8 of the Book of the Acts of the Apostles tells us the story of St. Philip converting an Ethiopian government official. That by itself is proof that Dawkins is wrong. Why bother to convert people who aren't human? I dare Dawkins to name one single pope or prominent Catholic or Protestant theologian who ever said blacks weren't human. Is there really no lie so ridiculous that Dawkins won't tell it?

Item 5: Essentialism

This Idea Must Die is a book of essays edited by a chap named John Brockman, and it contains an essay by Dawkins in which Dawkins criticizes an idea called "essentialism," which, according to Dawkins, is the idea that things found in nature can be neatly and clearly categorized. Dawkins says that is often not true. He is probably right about that, but then he goes overboard by claiming that the electoral college, which chooses American presidents, is a "manifestation of essentialist thinking. Florida must go wholly Republican or wholly Democrat – all twenty-nine Electoral College votes – even though the popular vote is a dead heat."

That is nonsense. The reason why every state except Maine and Nebraska has a winner-take-all system for allocating electoral votes is not because our state legislators believe in essentialism. It isn't even because the delegates at the Constitutional Convention in 1787 believed in essentialism. The state governments could easily get rid of the winner-take-all system if they wanted too, but in liberal states, the liberals think, "Why should we let the conservatives have any of our state's electoral votes? Let's have a winner-take-all system," while in conservative states, the conservatives think, "Why should we let the liberals have any of our state's electoral votes? Let's have a winner-take-all system." But Dawkins never thinks of that obvious fact.

And what about the toss-up states? Well, if a state has twenty-nine electoral votes, and the race there is close, then under the winner-take-all system, both major candidates will spend a lot of money in that state, and pander to the state's major industries and ethnic groups, because twenty-nine electoral votes are a major prize. But if electoral votes are allocated according to each candidate's percentage of the popular vote, then the winner will get only fifteen, sixteen or seventeen electoral votes, which is only a few more than the number the loser will get, so the state will not be a major prize, and so the major candidates will spend little money on advertising there and will not pander to the state's major industries and ethnic groups. Look at Florida. There are a lot of Jews in Florida, so presidential candidates go to Florida and promise they will support Israel to the hilt. There are a lot of Cuban-Americans in Florida, so presidential candidates go to Florida and brag about how tough they will be on Cuba. Sugar cane is a major crop in Florida, so presidential candidates go to Florida and promise to give the sugar growers what they want. NASA is a major employer in Florida, so presidential candidates go to Florida and promise to generously fund NASA. Meanwhile, the TV stations in Florida make big money by selling advertising time to the presidential candidates. None of these things would happen nearly to the extent they do now, if Florida was not a winner-take-all state.

To learn all this stuff, all Dawkins had to do was talk to a political science professor. Why didn't he? Does he feel no need to gather information before he shoots his mouth off?

Item 6: The Outrage at Gibeah

On page 241 of *The God Delusion* (page 273 of the paperback) Dawkins talks about the story of the Outrage at Gibeah, which is in chapter 19 of the Book of Judges in the Bible. A homeowner in the town of Gibeah takes into his house two houseguests, a male Levite and his concubine. During the night, a crowd gathers outside the house, demanding that the Levite be thrown out to them for gang rape. The homeowner offers the mob either the concubine or his own daughter. Rather than wait for an answer, the Levite simply grabs his concubine and shoves her out the door. The mob rapes her all night, and she dies.

Dawkins complains that that was an awful thing for the homeowner and the Levite to do. He fails to notice that the Bible does not say it was good. It merely records that that is what happened.

Next the Levite cuts the body of his concubine into twelve pieces and sends the pieces "throughout the territory of Israel." (Chapter 19, verse 29 of the Book of Judges.) Dawkins calls that "weirdness." The truth is that that was the Levite's way of notifying the people of Israel about this terrible crime, and asking that the perpetrators be punished. In the hardcover edition of his book, Dawkins fails to mention that. In the hardcover edition, Dawkins makes it sound like this was simply a pointless desecration of a corpse.

Next, in chapter 20 of the Book of Judges, eleven of the tribes of Israel hold a council and decide they must punish the men of Gibeah for this horrible crime. The tribe of Benjamin, however, disagrees, because the men of Gibeah belonged to the tribe of Benjamin. The Benjaminites refuse to hand over the murderers for execution, so the other eleven tribes assemble an army, invade the territory of Benjamin, and defeat the Benjaminite army.

In the paperback, but not in the hardcover edition, Dawkins writes that the Levite sent the pieces of his concubine's corpse throughout the land of Israel "to provoke revenge," and says the war between the

Israelites and the Benjaminites was "a war of vengeance." One feels astonished to read such talk. It is perfectly obvious that the murderers deserved to be punished. It would've been appalling if the Israelites had done nothing to punish the Benjaminites for what they had done. Why does Dawkins object to that? One is forced to conclude that Dawkins is the kind of leftist who cannot bear the thought of criminals being punished. Does he not know that if crime is not punished, it will become more common? Or does he not care?

Item 7: Dawkins Analyzes Chimps

On page 300-301 of *The God Delusion* (page 340-341 of the paperback) Dawkins makes an argument that is weird even by his standards. He is talking about abortion, and says we cannot give special "moral status" to human beings, because of "our evolutionary continuity with chimpanzees and, more distantly, with every species on the planet."

Mr. Dawkins, did you give that any serious thought at all before you wrote that? In a country that has national health insurance, do you really think the government should spend as much money to save the life of a chimp as it does to save the life of a human? If you and a chimp were in a spaceship, and some accident happened, and as a result of this accident there wasn't enough oxygen left for both you and the chimp to get back to Earth alive, would you really draw straws with the chimp and, if you lost, commit suicide so the chimp could have all the oxygen? Do you really think your moral right to life is no better than a chimp's? Those are all obvious questions, but Dawkins doesn't discuss any of them. Apparently he never thought of them.

Then Dawkins talks about *Australopithecus afarensis*, which he says is an extinct species of semi-humans. He asks what we would do if we found some of them alive today, in some remote part of the world. Would we consider them human? Believe it or not, he declares that he would not care about the answer to that question, because he thinks it just doesn't matter. Come off it, Mr. Dawkins. We would still have to decide whether they should be allowed to vote and serve on juries. Can't you see that? We would still have to decide whether they can own real estate and sign legally binding contracts. We would have to decide whether to outlaw job discrimination against them. We don't give someone a sentence of life in prison for killing a member of an endangered species. Would we give someone a sentence of life in prison for killing an *Australopithecus afarensis*? Did Dawkins truly never think of these obvious questions?

Item 8: Dawkins Lies About Benjamin Franklin

A few years ago, an American history professor named H.W. Brands wrote a biography of Benjamin Franklin called *The First American: The Life and Times of Benjamin Franklin*. On page 278, he tells the story of how Franklin's ship nearly sank when he traveled to England in 1757. After this incident, Franklin wrote a letter to his wife in which he joked, "Were I a Roman Catholic, perhaps I should on this occasion vow to build a chapel to some saint; but as I am not, if I were to vow at all, it should be to build a lighthouse." If you do an Internet search for the words Benjamin Franklin lighthouse church, you will see that some atheists claim Franklin said, "Lighthouses are more useful than churches," while debunkers say no, Franklin never said that, the claim that he said that is based on that joke he wrote in a letter to his wife after he nearly drowned.

On page 43 of *The God Delusion*, (page 64 of the paperback) Dawkins claims Benjamin Franklin said, "Lighthouses are more useful than churches." Dawkins doesn't mention any source of information for this alleged quote. Apparently he thinks his readers should just take his words on faith. Why does he want us to take his words on faith, but not Jesus's? On pages 306-308 (pages 346-348 of the paperback) he says we should never take anything on faith, but apparently he thinks he is such a wonderful guy that an exception should be made for his pronouncements. One has to suspect that Dawkins cites no source of information for this quote because he got it from some crackpot website, and he wants to hide that fact from his readers.

The truth is that we know quite a bit about Franklin's religious beliefs. The year before he died he discussed them at length in a letter to a man named Ezra Stiles. "Here is my creed," Franklin said. "I believe in one God, creator of the universe. That he governs it by his providence.

That he ought to be worshipped. That the most acceptable service we render to him is doing good to his other children. That the soul of man is immortal, and will be treated with justice in another life respecting its conduct in this." He went on to say that he did not know whether Jesus was divine, and joked that because he was very old, he would probably find out for certain soon enough. (Endnote 19.)

Let us also remember that at the Constitutional Convention, a few weeks after it began, Franklin suggested that the delegates start each session with prayer. He said, "How has it happened, sir, that we have not hitherto once thought of humbly applying to the Father of Lights to illuminate our understandings? ... And the longer I live the more convincing proofs I see of this truth, that God governs in the affairs of men. And if a sparrow cannot fall to the ground without His notice, is it probable that an empire can rise without His aid?" (Endnote 20.) We also know that Franklin once told a friend who was planning to write an anti-Christian book that the only thing such a book could possibly achieve would be to raise the crime rate. "If men are so wicked as we now see them with religion," Franklin asked, "what would they be if without it?" (Endnote 21.)

Can we trust Brands's book? The reviewer in the *New York Times* thought the book was boring, but did not question its accuracy.

Brands's book was published in 2000. Dawkins could've consulted it while writing *The God Delusion*, if he had cared about giving his readers the truth. Is Dawkins really so dimwitted that it never occurred to him that if he wanted to find out about Benjamin Franklin's religious beliefs, he should consult a biography written by a reputable history professor? No, he can't be that dimwitted. He must have been trying to deceive his readers.

Item 9: Dawkins Lies About Thomas Jefferson

Dawkins also gives his readers a false impression of the beliefs of Thomas Jefferson. On page 42 of *The God Delusion*, (page 63 of the paperback) Dawkins quotes Jefferson as saying, "To talk of immaterial existences is to talk of nothings. To say that the human soul, angels, god are immaterial, is to say they are nothings, or that there is no god, no angels, no soul. I cannot reason otherwise." Dawkins says this sounds like Jefferson was an agnostic.

It is true that Jefferson said that, in a letter to John Adams in 1820. The full text of the letter can be found on pages 1440-1445 of the book *Thomas Jefferson / Writings* edited by the prominent historian Merrill D. Peterson for the Library of America series. But Dawkins leaves out the context. That passage occurs in a very long paragraph, and when you read what came before and after that passage, you see that Jefferson is merely arguing that there can be no such things as "immaterial existences" and that therefore God must have a body, and the human soul must be a physical thing, "an etherial gas," as Jefferson calls it on page 1444.

Is Dawkins really so lazy that he couldn't be bothered to read the entire letter? Maybe, but it is more likely that he found that quote on some atheist website and never even wondered what the context was.

Then on page 43, (page 64 of the paperback) Dawkins claims Jefferson once said, "Christianity is the most perverted system that ever shone on man." He doesn't say where he found that quote. I couldn't find it in *Thomas Jefferson / Writings*, nor in any book about Jefferson, so I suspect it is just a phony quote that Dawkins found on some crackpot website. If Jefferson actually said something that drastic, why doesn't Dawkins tell his readers where they can look it up? Why does he expect them to take his word on faith instead?

We know, beyond all doubt, that Jefferson said things that were quite different. Look at page 1458 of *Thomas Jefferson / Writings*, and you will see that in a letter to a friend in 1822, Jefferson wrote, "The doctrines of Jesus are simple, and tend all to the happiness of man. 1. That there is one only God, and he all perfect. 2. That there is a future state of rewards and punishments. 3. That to love God with all thy heart and thy neighbor as thyself, is the sum of religion. These are the great points on which he endeavored to reform the religion of the Jews." Then on page 1459, in the same letter, Jefferson writes, "Had the doctrines of Jesus been preached always as pure as they came from his lips, the whole civilized world would now have been Christian."

It is important to remember though, that Jefferson detested the ideas of the famous Protestant theologian John Calvin, and frequently said so. For example, on page 1466 of *Thomas Jefferson / Writings*, in a letter to John Adams in 1823, Jefferson denounced Calvin and said, "He was indeed an Atheist, which I can never be; or rather his religion was Daemonism. If ever a man worshipped a false god, he did." He goes on to say that nobody needs the Bible to tell them God exists, that the existence of the laws of physics and the existence of a harmonious, well-balanced universe prove there must be a Creator.

On page 43 of *The God Delusion*, (page 64 of the paperback) Dawkins writes that Jefferson may have been an atheist. As one can see from the above quote, that is definitely not true. Why in the world would Jefferson, in his old age, lie about his beliefs to his old friend John Adams? Once again, Dawkins is shooting off his mouth without bothering to gather any evidence first.

On page 354 of *The God Delusion*, (page 396 of the paperback) Dawkins writes that Jefferson "seems to have believed in no kind of afterlife." Once again, Dawkins is wrong. On page 1469 of *Thomas Jefferson / Writings*, Jefferson tells John Adams in a letter in 1823 that he looks forward to seeing him again soon in Heaven. He said the same thing in another letter to Adams later the same year. (See page

1478.) He said the same thing in a letter in 1824 to a friend named John Cartwright. (See page 1496.) How many times does he have to say it before people like Dawkins will take him seriously? We also have Jefferson's daughter's testimony that in the last weeks of his life, Jefferson told her he was looking forward to seeing her mother soon in Heaven. (Endnote 22.) And finally, to top it all off, not long before his death, Jefferson wrote a letter to a friend's son, full of advice on how to live, and said, "Adore God. Reverence and cherish your parents. Love your neighbor as yourself, and your country more than yourself. Be just. Be true. Murmur not at the ways of Providence. So shall the life into which you have entered, be the portal to one of eternal and ineffable bliss." (See page 1499.)

Dawkins says on page 354 of *The God Delusion* (pages 396-397 of the paperback) that in his old age, Jefferson said he was approaching death with "neither hope nor fear." Jefferson did indeed say that at least once, and naturally one wonders how to square that with all his talk about the afterlife. Maybe he felt no fear simply because he was sure he had committed no serious sins. And as for "hope," perhaps he just meant that he had no hope that he was going to be able to put off death much longer. Or maybe saying he had neither hope nor fear was just his way of saying he felt completely serene, willing to accept whatever came his way.

The way people use words tends to change as the centuries go by. Anyone who reads Shakespeare's plays knows that. Look at the way John Brown, in his famous speech at his trial, said, "I am yet too young to understand that God is any respecter of persons." What he meant by that was that God wants the law to apply equally to everyone, regardless of color, but nobody today would phrase that idea the way Brown phrased it. (Endnote 23.) Or look at the fact that Benjamin Franklin once said, "Experience keeps a dear school, yet fools will learn in no other." (Endnote 24.) By "dear" he meant "expensive," but I bet many people today would have no idea what he was talking about. We don't use the word "dear" that way anymore. Look at the fact that people in the United States used to use the word "rum" to mean "strange." You can see a quote like that from Oliver Wendell Holmes Jr. in an article by Peter Brown in the October 26, 2017 *New York Review of Books*. Nobody in the United States uses the word "rum" that way anymore. And look at the way Charles Darwin, in chapter 7 of his book *The Descent of Man*, talks about "a full-blooded negro with whom I happened once to be intimate." Now days, of course, being "intimate" with someone means engaging in some kind of sexual activity with him or her, but apparently it did not mean that back then.

So perhaps Jefferson used the word "hope" in a way different than the way a modern American would use it. Otherwise, I cannot see how one can square his "neither hope nor fear" statement with the fact that Jefferson definitely talked about the afterlife in his letters and seems to have had no doubt that there was one.

To get the truth about Jefferson's religious beliefs, all Dawkins had to do was get a copy of a good, scholarly biography of the man (many have been written) and go to the index and look up the pages where Jefferson's religious views are discussed. Why didn't he? Because he didn't want to tell his readers the truth.

Item 10: Dawkins Lies About Nuclear War

On page 302 of *The God Delusion*, (page 341 of the paperback) Dawkins claims that some Christians "actually yearn for nuclear war." He presents not one single scrap of evidence to support this claim. He doesn't name one single Christian clergyman who has ever said "I would be happy if nuclear war broke out tomorrow," or anything like that. He wants his readers to just take this accusation on faith.

There certainly are Christians who believe the world will end with a big nuclear war, but it should be obvious that predicting something and hoping for it are two different things. Astronomers, after all, predict that the sun will eventually become a red giant, making life on Earth impossible, but I'm not going to accuse them of actually wanting that to happen.

An Israeli journalist named Gershom Gorenberg wrote a book years ago called *The End of Days: Fundamentalism and the Struggle for the Temple Mount*. In it he talks about Christians who believe in a theological system called dispensational premillennialism. This system is the basis for the famous "Left Behind" series of novels by Tim LaHaye and Jerry B. Jenkins, which describe events leading up to the end of the world, and this system is also, I suspect, what Dawkins is talking about when he claims that some Christians "yearn for nuclear war." But Gorenberg and the "Left Behind" novels make clear that people who believe in dispensational premillennialism definitely do NOT "yearn for nuclear war." They believe that they, and all good Christians, someday, in an instant, will vanish from Earth and be taken up into Heaven in an event called "the Rapture." Only seven years AFTER the Rapture will a big war break out to end the world. Therefore, if a nuclear war broke out tomorrow, they would say this is definitely NOT the end of the world, because the Rapture hasn't occurred yet. They make it very clear that the Rapture must come first. (Endnote 25.)

Why does Dawkins shoot his mouth off about what this or that group of Christians believes when it is obvious that he has not even bothered to talk to them or read any of their books to find out what they believe?

If you want to talk about people desiring mass death, however, look at a scientist named Eric Pianka. He has publicly declared that he would be glad if an epidemic wiped out 90 percent of the human race, as long as he and his buddies were among the survivors, because that would cut down on the amount of environmental damage done by the human race. (Endnote 26.) I bet he is not the only environmentalist who thinks that way, and I bet there are some who would not mind being among the dead, who would consider that a price worth paying in order to save the whales, the gorillas, the elephants, and the rest of the environment. But Dawkins never talks about scientists who think that way, even though this is a serious problem. It is easy to imagine that biochemists will someday know so much about viruses that a terrorist group will be able to create a deadly new virus, vaccinate the members of the group against it, and then turn it loose on the world, thereby killing almost everyone on Earth. As I said earlier, a chap named John Brockman has edited a book called *What Should We Be Worried About?* and on pages 12-13 of that book, a prominent scientist named Martin Rees says he is worried that "synthetic biology" technology will drastically increase the possibility of biological terrorism. It seems possible that soon, even people who aren't well educated will be able to create new viruses.

And look at the fact that the atheists who run *Esquire* magazine rejoiced when the famous cartoonist Charles Schulz died, because Schulz was a Christian. Look at the January 2001 issue of *Esquire*. There is a cartoon strip on page 62 in which Charlie Brown, Snoopy and the rest of Schulz's characters rejoice because Schulz is dead, because he can no longer control them and so now they are free to do what they want. (What they want, according to *Esquire*, is to engage in sexual behavior. Plus, Charlie Brown gets revenge for years of insults by punching Lucy.)

This gloating over the death of an utterly harmless man leads to the conclusion that the atheists who run *Esquire* would be glad if every Christian on Earth suddenly fell over dead. Is Dawkins going to criticize them for that?

Or how about this fact: George Orwell was an atheist, and he said in June 1942 that he hoped World War Two would NOT end soon. I know it seems impossible to believe that anyone would say something so outrageous, but that really is what he said in his diary. (Endnote 27.) In June 1942, Orwell attended a dinner party and met Sir Stafford Cripps, a high-ranking British government official. Cripps said he thought the war might end in just a few months, because British intelligence believed the Nazis were running out of food and supplies. Orwell said that would be "a disaster pure and simple," because a long war was necessary to produce a "real upheaval" in Great Britain that would usher in a socialist government, which, in Orwell's opinion, was what Great Britain really needed.

All over Britain, and all over the world, friends and relatives of soldiers and sailors were praying for the war to end soon, so their loved ones could come home safe and sound, but this atheist Orwell was hoping for a long war with many deaths, so his political dream might come true. How cold-hearted can you get?

And of course, even though Orwell got the long bloody war that he wanted, his dream of a socialist Britain that would abolish private property and destroy capitalism never came true.

Item 11: Dawkins Lies About George H.W. Bush

On page 43 of *The God Delusion* (page 65 of the paperback), Dawkins first claims President George H.W. Bush once said, when asked if atheists can be good citizens, "No, I don't know that atheists should be considered as citizens, nor should they be considered patriots." But then, out of the other side of his mouth, Dawkins admits that quote may not be "accurate." His source for the quote is some atheist publication, and he admits that nobody else has ever reported Bush saying that or anything like that.

Maybe I should act like Dawkins. Maybe I should claim Dawkins once said, "I used to be involved in Ponzi schemes. It gave me great pleasure to swindle people." Then a few sentences later, I could protect myself from a libel suit by saying, "Well, that quote may not be accurate."

The simple fact is that if George H.W. Bush had ever said anything that outrageous, it would've gotten a lot of attention in the press, and the editorial boards of the *New York Times*, the *Washington Post*, the *Nation*, the *New Republic*, and many other newspapers and magazines would've sternly criticized him for it. Therefore we can be certain that quote is false.

Item 12: Edward O. Wilson

Nowhere in *The God Delusion* does Dawkins condemn, or even mention, the moral philosophy of Edward O. Wilson, even though he mentions Wilson on page 347 (page 389 of the paperback) and calls him "great." Wilson is a famous Harvard biologist and is not the least bit religious. He said in his book *Consilience*, in the chapter called "Ethics and Religion," that he believes there are no eternal moral truths, that morality is a fabrication of the human mind, that an action is immoral only if people think it is. Therefore one must conclude that Wilson would say that if most people on Earth want to exterminate the Jews or gays or any other group, there is nothing immoral about that. If you said to him, "It is wrong to kill people just because they belong to this or that ethnic group," he would reply, "If that was true, that would be an eternal moral truth, but I have already proved that there are no eternal moral truths." *Consilience* got quite a bit of attention when it was published. Many newspapers and magazines reviewed it. Is it possible that Dawkins never read it and has no idea that Wilson thinks there are no eternal moral truths? Perhaps, but I think it is more likely that Dawkins knows that perfectly well but simply prefers to not discuss Wilson's philosophy because he doesn't want his readers to know that a brilliant atheist scientist such as Wilson thinks morality is a joke and that eternal moral truths don't exist. Dawkins is afraid that if people hear about Wilson's views, they'll be horrified. Dawkins is afraid that people will see that if atheism becomes more common, more and more people will think like Wilson.

Morning, noon, and night, Dawkins will bash Christianity, but when will he utter a word critical of Wilsonism? Never. That he tries to cover up.

I'm not the only one to have noticed this. *The God Delusion* was reviewed in the October 22, 2006 issue of the *New York Times Book Review*, and the reviewer mentioned that Wilson believes morality is a meaningless concept, an "illusion," and that Dawkins says nothing to oppose that idea.

Item 13: Is Morality Logical?

In the July 2007 issue of *Scientific American* magazine, on page 90, Dawkins says we must get rid of "irrational beliefs." He wants everyone to be logical.

Several years ago, in the Baltic Sea, a ship called the *Estonia* sank one night and around eight hundred people drowned. There were enough life jackets on board for everyone, but they were in lockers located all around the deck. The *Estonia* began listing severely soon after it started to sink, so, in the dark, with high waves crashing into the ship, it was not safe to go to the low side of the ship to get a life jacket from one of the lockers there. So some people simply beat up other people and grabbed the life jackets right off their bodies. (You can read about this incident on page 156 of William Langewiesche's book, *The Outlaw Sea*.) Why did they do it? Because it was the logical thing to do, if you are an atheist. If there is no afterlife and my life is in danger, why I should I not do absolutely anything to stay alive?

That, of course, proves that logic is not the same thing as morality. Why does Dawkins never think of that? If you are faced with a moral question, you should turn to Jesus, not to logic. I assume Dawkins would say it is terrible to beat up a 12-year-old girl on a sinking ship and steal her life jacket, but what logical reason could he possibly give for saying that? There is none.

Similarly, why not invest your money in tobacco companies? Obviously it is immoral to make money by pushing an addictive drug, but there is no law against it, you aren't going to be punished for it on this Earth in any way, and the profits are good, so it is the logical thing to do. Obviously it is immoral to invest your money in companies that use slave labor in foreign countries, but if all you care about is logic, why not do it? The profits are good, and you aren't going to be punished for it on this Earth.

Obviously you can make a ton of money by writing political books that are full of lies, and that is why so many people do it. The famous filmmaker Oliver Stone made millions of dollars by telling people the preposterous lie that President Kennedy was killed by a massive right-wing conspiracy. What logical reason could Dawkins give him to forgo that opportunity?

Next, let's look at a massive study of American religion carried out by Robert D. Putnam, a professor of Public Policy at Harvard University, a former president of the American Political Science Association, and one of America's most highly-esteemed social scientists, and David E. Campbell, a professor of political science at the University of Notre Dame. They published their findings in 2010 in a book called *American Grace: How Religion Divides and Unites Us*. On pages 445-465, they report that the least religious people give a lot less money to charity, even to secular charities, than the most religious people do. Obviously, they do that because of logic. If I'm an atheist, why should I care about people starving in Africa? How is it going to benefit me if I save their lives? Obviously, it won't. On the contrary, if they stay alive, they may immigrate to the United States and start competing with me and my friends for jobs. Why would I want that?

You don't have to just take my word for it. Steven Pinker, a famous Harvard psychology professor who is not the least bit religious, discussed this question on pages 245-247 of his book *The Blank Slate: The Modern Denial of Human Nature*, and came to the same conclusion that I have reached: that there is no logical reason to help strangers. Evolution, he says, did not design people to do that, because any animal that spends its time and energy helping others will have less time and energy to help itself, which will decrease its chances of surviving and reproducing.

A wealthy Swede named Raoul Wallenberg went to Hungary during World War Two and used various tricks to save 30,000 Jews from the Nazis, risking his life repeatedly in the process. All the Jews whom he saved were strangers. Doing this benefited him in no way. In fact, it got him killed, in the end. You can read about him in Wikipedia, and several books have been written about him too. Clearly there was never a less logical man than Raoul Wallenberg.

When the Montreal police went on strike in 1969, a crime wave ensued. A doctor killed a burglar who broke into his house, six banks in Montreal were robbed in one day, and there was widespread looting of stores. The city government had to call in the army. Why did this happen? Because when there is little or no chance of being caught, stealing is the logical thing to do. (Endnote 28.)

Or look at the fact that surely Dawkins would say it is bad for a fellow to lie to a woman in order to get her into bed, but one has to admit, it happens all the time, and the men who do it think they're being perfectly logical. Remember that scene in Spike Lee's movie *School Daze* in which a nerd, played by Lee himself, asks a promiscuous guy what the secret is to having a busy sex life, and the promiscuous guy says "Tell them what they want to hear. Lie your butt off."

Look at how common it is for politicians to take bribes. Why does that happen? Because the profits are huge, and the chances of getting punished for it (on Earth, anyway) are almost zero.

Look at King Leopold II of Belgium. Why did he, and so many other colonialists, invade weak countries and steal everything they could get? Because that was the logical thing to do. It made them rich. Why did so many people violate the United Nations sanctions against Saddam Hussein? Because there was a ton of money to be made by doing that, and violators saw no logical reason to care about the fact that they were helping Saddam stay in power and continue to treat his people like slaves.

I would never say we should believe something just because Einstein said it, but still, many people, including Dawkins, have a high regard for old Albert, so it might be worthwhile to listen to his thoughts on the subject. Unlike Dawkins, he freely admitted that he felt no need to be logical all the time. "I believe in the brotherhood of man and the uniqueness of the individual," he said near the end of his life, and he went on to say this:

> "But if you ask me to prove what I believe, I can't. You know them to be true but you could spend a whole lifetime without being able to prove them. The mind can proceed only so far upon what it knows and can prove. There comes a point where the mind takes a higher plane of knowledge, but can never prove how it got there. All great discoveries have involved such a leap." (Endnote 29.)

And yet Dawkins sits there and says everyone should be logical all the time. Is he really unable to see that relentless logic would make this world a nightmare?

Item 14: Dawkins Lies About Charles Darwin

In a footnote on page 62 of his book *The Greatest Show on Earth*, Dawkins says Darwin didn't talk about a struggle for survival between races, the way Hitler did. "For Darwin," Dawkins says, "the struggle for existence was a struggle between individuals within a species, <u>not</u> between species, races, or other groups."

Dawkins is wrong again. Look at what Darwin said once in a letter to a friend:

> "I could show fight on natural selection having done and doing more for the progress of civilization than you seem inclined to admit. Remember what risk the nations of Europe ran, not so many centuries ago, of being overwhelmed by the Turks, and how ridiculous such an idea now is! The more civilized so-called Caucasian races have beaten the Turkish hollow in the struggle for existence. Looking to the world at no very distant date, what an endless number of the lower races will have been eliminated by the higher races throughout the world." (Endnote 30.)

You see? When "lower races" were "eliminated" by "higher races," Darwin thought that was an example of "the progress of civilization." Obviously there is not much difference between that and the way Hitler thought.

And that wasn't a one-shot fluke. Another time, Darwin wrote to a friend, "It is very true what you say about the higher races of men, when high enough, will have spread & exterminated whole nations." (Endnote 31.)

And there is more. Look at chapter 5 of Darwin's book *The Descent of Man*, and you will see a passage in which he calls the Irish a bunch of lazy idiots, much inferior to the Scots. Look at chapter 6 of the same book, and you will see a passage where he says blacks are more closely related to gorillas than whites are, and predicts that the blacks will eventually be exterminated.

So either Dawkins is lying about Darwin, or else he shot his mouth off about Darwin without bothering to learn about him first.

Item 15: NASA

On page 316 of his book *The Greatest Show on Earth*, Dawkins says the Apollo moon landings are "one of those achievements that makes me proud to be human."

I'll never forget a cartoon that the famous political cartoonist Herb Block produced shortly after the moon landing: a starving child holding a bowl of rocks and saying "Thank you sir. They're very nice moon rocks." That was the spirit of the Apollo missions: ignore the needs of the human race, concentrate on a trivial, Buck Rogers fantasy. Dawkins applauds that.

Item 16: Dawkins Lies About the Bosnian War

On page 1 of *The God Delusion*, (page 23 of the paperback), Dawkins blames religion for "Serb/Croat/Muslim massacres."

Okay, let's look at that episode. In the Bosnian War in the 1990s, around 200,000 Bosnians were murdered by Serbs. (Endnote 32.) Some people like to blame this slaughter on Christianity, but the truth is that there is no reason to believe Christians were to blame for what happened in Bosnia. For proof, read the book *Origins of a Catastrophe* by Warren Zimmermann, the last American ambassador to Yugoslavia. Slobodan Milosevic, the Serb dictator, was to blame for the war, Zimmermann says on page viii and on page 251. Without him, it wouldn't have happened, and he was an atheist. (Endnote 33.) Except on rare occasions, for political purposes, Milosevic never set foot inside a church in his life. He had a successful career as a communist party official in Yugoslavia in the days when communists were required to be atheists.

The average Serb was not enthusiastic about the war in Bosnia, and the Serb soldiers in the regular army did not want to fight in it. That is why paramilitaries, who were often convicted criminals recruited out of prisons, did most of the fighting. Their motivation was financial, not religious. They were told if they volunteered to go fight in Bosnia, they would be allowed to loot Muslim homes. (Endnote 34.) I've never heard of any evidence that these paramilitary hoodlums were religious. Dawkins, Christopher Hitchens, and the rest of the militant atheists certainly never mention any.

Franjo Tudjman, the Croat leader, was also partly to blame for the war, but he too seems to have been an atheist. He was a communist for years, when the Yugoslav communist party required its members to be atheists. (Endnote 35.) As communism collapsed, he joined the

Catholic Church and got himself elected president of Croatia. One has to wonder if his conversion was sincere.

Both Milosevic and Tudjman used TV and newspapers to stir up hatred against other ethnic groups in Yugoslavia. (Endnote 36.) Before the war, friendships and marriages between Serbs, Croats and Bosnian Muslims had been common (endnote 37) but it seems to be a simple fact of human nature that most people believe the news reports they see on TV, and clergymen seem to be no different than anyone else in this regard. Milosevic told his people, every day, that innocent Serbs were being butchered in Croatia and Bosnia. He had film clips of dead bodies shown on TV and said those were murdered Serbs. Tudjman made similar claims. The common people, and most clergymen too, believed it. They had no other sources of information. All over the world, most people are easily persuaded that their group is being unfairly oppressed. As I said above, the common people in Serbia did not become enthusiastic about the war, but the propaganda induced them to not oppose it either.

Muslim blunders also contributed to the problem. Ambassador Zimmerman says before the war in Bosnia started, he tried to convince the Bosnian Muslim leaders that they should negotiate with the Bosnian Serbs and try to reach a compromise that both sides could live with, but the Bosnian Muslim leaders refused. They were sure such negotiations would be an idiotic waste of time, that no reasonable compromise was possible. (Endnote 38.) During World War II, thousands of Serbs were massacred by Croats, who sometimes were assisted by Bosnian Muslims. That is why Bosnian Serbs were afraid of coming under Muslim rule. Any sensible Muslim leader would've tried to calm their fears, but the Bosnian Muslim leaders refused to even try.

Thomas L. Friedman, a famous *New York Times* foreign policy commentator, agreed with Zimmerman's assessment. Friedman sized up the situation and concluded that the Bosnian Muslim leaders had brought their troubles on themselves. (Endnote 39.)

Dawkins never mentions that Milosevic was an atheist, and that Tudjman probably was too. He doesn't want his readers to think about that. For decades, Yugoslavia was officially a communist atheist country, but Dawkins talks as though there wasn't a single atheist in the whole place. He can't bear to face the truth.

Item 17: Photographs

On page 1 of *The God Delusion*, (page 23 of the paperback) Dawkins praises an ad he once saw, that said "Imagine a world without religion," with a picture of the New York City skyline with the World Trade Center still standing. One could just as easily symbolize a world without religion with that famous photo of a pile of human skulls found in a prison run by the Khmer Rouge, an atheist movement, but Dawkins apparently never thought of that.

Item 18: John Lennon

On page 2 of *The God Delusion*, (page 24 of the paperback) Dawkins says "Imagine" by John Lennon, which advocates atheism, is a "magnificent song."

One can only laugh at such talk. The melody of "Imagine" is just a nice little lullaby, and there is nothing terribly imaginative or poetic about the lyrics. If "Imagine" is "magnificent," then so is a can of beans. Dawkins's statement reminds me of the time George Orwell complained about communist literary critics who were willing to praise any idiotic novel as long as it was written by a communist.

You don't have to just take my word for it. Lennon's biographer Philip Norman has said "Imagine" is "in many respects, one of his least inventive songs. ... Nor are the lyrics anywhere near the standard he reached in, say, 'Norwegian Wood.'" (Endnote 40.) Although in the end, Norman, a loyal fan, says he likes "Imagine."

I could easily compile a list of two hundred songs that are far better than "Imagine." Here, in no particular order, are just twenty of them.

1. "Sunday Morning Coming Down" by Kris Kristofferson.
2. "Stairway to Heaven" by Led Zeppelin.
3. "A Day in the Life" by the Beatles.
4. "Here's Where the Story Ends" by the Sundays.
5. "A Change Is Gonna Come" by Sam Cooke.
6. "Biko" by Peter Gabriel.
7. "Running to Stand Still" by U2.
8. "Fast Car" by Tracy Chapman.
9. "One" by U2.
10. "The Bewlay Brothers" by David Bowie.
11. "Sunshine" by Jonathan Edwards.
12. "Maggie's Farm" by Bob Dylan.
13. "Dignity" by Bob Dylan.
14. "The Ghost of Tom Joad" by Bruce Springsteen.

15. "Eminence Front" by the Who.

16. "Come As You Are" by Nirvana.

17. "Don't Look Now" by Creedence Clearwater Revival.

18. "Bridge Over Troubled Water" by Simon and Garfunkel.

19. "Captain Kennedy" by Neil Young.

20. "After the Gold Rush" by Neil Young.

Compared to masterpieces like those, "Imagine" sounds like something a 12-year-old wrote.

And, of course, the lyrics of "Imagine" are just simplistic utopianism. The song asks us to "Imagine no possessions." That is a reference to the old socialist idea that private property should be abolished, that everything on Earth should be owned in common by everyone. There used to be socialist farming communes in Israel, called kibbutzes, that took this principle very seriously indeed. In some kibbutzes, people didn't even own their own clothes. If your clothes were dirty, you went to a storage building next to the laundry, and the clerk on duty would give you some clean clothes that were your size. (Endnote 41.)

So, if Dawkins loves the song "Imagine" so much, does that mean he is going to give away all his money and join a socialist farming commune? Don't hold your breath waiting for that to happen. Lennon, of course, never did that either. He was living in luxury when he died, with a net worth of $250 million. Just a few days before he died, *The Isthmus*, a left-wing weekly newspaper in Madison, Wisconsin, sarcastically referred to him as "John Lennon, the famous real estate tycoon." Once, when Lennon was grumbling about his wife's extravagant spending, his friend Neil Aspinall said, "Imagine no possessions, John," and Lennon replied, "It's only a bloody song." (Endnote 42.) Lennon himself didn't take the song seriously. Why should anyone else?

No, it is obvious that Dawkins likes "Imagine" only because it has an atheist message. Apparently he will praise any mediocre thing, as long as it has an atheist message.

Dawkins might be surprised to hear that even though Lennon was an atheist, he believed in astrology. In December 1974, more than a year after he wrote "Imagine," Lennon refused to attend a meeting to sign some important legal documents because his astrologer told him it was a bad day for signing documents. (Endnote 43.) Then in 1980, when he decided to go on a sea voyage on a rented yacht, he picked the crew members by using astrology and numerology. (Endnote 44.)

There's a sordid footnote to Lennon's life. A few days before he died, he filed an affidavit in a lawsuit in which he swore that "I and the three other former Beatles have plans to stage a reunion concert, to be recorded, filmed and marketed around the world." That wasn't true. Lennon tried to get Paul McCartney to file a similar affidavit, and Paul wouldn't do it. So apparently one of the last things this atheist Lennon did on Earth was commit perjury. (Endnote 45.) Imagine that.

Item 19: Carl Sagan's Babbling

On page 12 of *The God Delusion*, (page 32-33 of the paperback) Dawkins approvingly quotes Carl Sagan as saying:

> "How is it that hardly any major religion has looked at science and concluded, 'This is better than we thought! The Universe is much bigger than our prophets said, grander, more subtle, more elegant'? Instead they say, 'No, no, no! My god is a little god, and I want him to stay that way.' A religion, old or new, that stressed the magnificence of the Universe as revealed by modern science might be able to draw forth reserves of reverence and awe hardly tapped by the conventional faiths."

What Dawkins doesn't realize is that that is surely one of the most asinine statements that Sagan ever made. Sagan is assuming that the prophets' mission was to talk about the universe. That isn't even close to being true. Their mission was to talk about morality and justice and loyalty to God. And what does Sagan mean when he says some people want God to be "a little god"? I've never heard anyone say that. Obviously Sagan means that to be a metaphor for something, but for what? He never makes that clear. He seems to be saying that clergymen should talk more about astronomy. Why? What makes him think people go to church eager to hear about astronomy? I see no evidence for that. It sounds like Sagan was one of those guys who love their favorite subject so much that they find it impossible to imagine that anyone would not be interested in it, like those people who bore you to death by talking endlessly about golf.

Item 20: Albert Einstein

On pages 15-19 of *The God Delusion*, (page 35-39 of the paperback) Dawkins talks on and on about what a great guy he thinks Einstein was. He never mentions that Einstein was a cold-blooded murderer.

Here are the facts. Einstein lived in Germany during World War One and did military research with the goal of helping the German government win the war. You can read about this on pages 399-402 of Albrecht Folsing's book, *Albert Einstein: A Biography*, translated and abridged by Ewald Osers and published by Penguin Books in 1998. It is also mentioned in Frederic Golden's article about Einstein on pages 62-67 of *Time* magazine, December 31, 1999.

This would not be strange if Einstein was simply a patriotic German citizen, trying to help his country, but the truth is that he was no such thing. In September 1915 and again in August 1917 he made his views perfectly clear to his friend Romain Rolland. He said he wanted Germany to lose the war, because he thought Germany needed reform, and would never reform itself unless it was defeated. (Endnote 46.) He knew perfectly well that Germany had started the war for no good reason and that justice was not on Germany's side. In a letter to a friend, he said he thought it was amusing to hear other scientists, in the lunchroom at the institute where he worked, straining to try to explain why the world hated Germany so much. To Einstein, and indeed to any sensible person, the explanation was obvious: Germany was hated because Germany had started the war for no good reason. But most German scientists were so nationalistic that they could not bear to admit that. (Endnote 47.)

With regard to Einstein's military research for the kaiser, Albrecht Folsing, one of Einstein's biographers, writes, "it seems odd that, as a convinced pacifist, Einstein was evidently indifferent to the military implications of such work." (Endnote 48.) Folsing is wrong. It is not odd. Einstein was neither a Christian nor a Judaist. He did not believe in the immortality of the soul, and he had no fear of Hell, so even though he knew justice was not on Germany's side, he believed that the chance that he would be punished in any way for doing military research to help Germany was negligible, and he knew he could make some money by doing it, so he saw no reason not to. The fact that he was working to kill innocent men who were merely fighting to defend their countries against German aggression obviously meant nothing to him, as long as he could make money by killing them.

Just like a Mafia hit man, he was perfectly willing to kill total strangers who were doing no harm, as long as he was payed enough for his time and trouble.

His attitude continued after the war. His work on gyrocompasses resulted in a contract which gave him three percent of the sale price of each gyrocompass sold, and three percent of any revenue from licenses. When Mussolini bought Einstein's gyrocompasses for his navy, there is no record of Einstein objecting. (Endnote 49.)

And, remarkably, even Hitler bought Einstein's gyrocompasses. In January 1940, months after World War Two had started, Einstein wrote a letter to the Dutch firm that handled sales of the gyrocompasses. (The Netherlands at that time had not yet been invaded by Hitler.) Did the letter request that sales to Germany be halted? No. Instead Einstein complained that his royalty check had not arrived. He wanted his money. (Endnote 50.)

Adultery is small potatoes compared to murder, but it is still worth mentioning that Einstein was an adulterer too. Once he became famous, many women threw themselves at him, and he saw no reason to turn them all down. This hurt his wife's feelings, but he didn't care. (Endnote 51.)

So why does Dawkins lavish praise on Einstein? Once again, Dawkins can't be bothered to gather facts before he shoots his mouth off.

Item 21: Dawkins Lies About Ireland

On page 21 of *The God Delusion*, (page 43 of the paperback), Dawkins says it is dishonest that Irish Republican Army killers are called "nationalists" instead of Catholics.

Why? When has any Catholic bishop expressed approval of the violence committed by the IRA? Never that I've heard, and Dawkins mentions no such example. The IRA killers are called nationalists because they want to end British rule in Northern Ireland and establish a united Ireland. Doesn't that sound like Irish nationalism? It sure does to me.

Look at this statement that the Catholic bishops of Northern Ireland issued in September 1971.

> "In Northern Ireland at the present time there is a small group of people who are trying to secure a united Ireland by the use of force. One has only to state this fact in all its stark simplicity to see the absurdity of the idea. Who in his sane senses wants to bomb a million Protestants into a united Ireland? At times, the people behind this campaign will talk of defence. (sic) But ... their bombs have killed innocent people, including women and girls. Their campaign is bringing shame and disgrace on noble and just causes." (Endnote 52.)

But don't hold your breath waiting for Dawkins to quote that statement. That would be honesty, and why on Earth would Dawkins want to be honest?

Item 22: Dawkins Lies About Yugoslavia Again

On page 21 of *The God Delusion*, (page 43 of the paperback), Dawkins once again blames the fighting in Yugoslavia in the 1990s on religion. Once again he fails to mention that Milosevic, who instigated it all, was an atheist. Somehow that escapes his notice.

Item 23: Dawkins Gets Hoaxed

On page 25 of the hardcover edition of *The God Delusion*, Dawkins claims that some Muslim protestors in Britain in 2006 carried a banner that said "Behead those who say Islam is a violent religion." He points out that that is a self-contradictory thing to say, but he fails to say where he read that the Muslim protestors did that. Once again, he wants us to just take his word on faith. I suspect it's a hoax, that it never really happened. It sounds to me like something a comedian would make up.

In the paperback edition, Dawkins omitted that claim. I suspect someone proved to him that it was bogus.

Item 24: Randolph Churchill

On page 31 of *The God Delusion*, (page 51 of the paperback), Dawkins quotes Randolph Churchill, Winston Churchill's son, criticizing Christianity. Dawkins seems to think we should be impressed by that. I can't imagine why. Randolph Churchill was a short-tempered and remarkably obnoxious alcoholic who never amounted to a hill of beans. (Endnote 53.) Why does his opinion deserve any respect?

Item 25: Dawkins Lies About Thomas Jefferson Again

On page 31 of the hardcover edition of *The God Delusion*, Dawkins claims Thomas Jefferson once said, "The Christian God is a being of terrific character – cruel, vindictive, capricious, and unjust." Dawkins eventually admitted that was a misquote, and he didn't put it in the paperback edition. Instead, on page 51 of the paperback edition, he claims that Jefferson made those comments about "the God of Moses."

One wonders how Dawkins came to make that mistake.

So to repeat, on page 51 of the paperback, Dawkins says Jefferson described "the God of Moses" as "a being of terrific character – cruel, vindictive, capricious and unjust." Jefferson did indeed say that, but once again, Dawkins is giving his readers a false impression. Jefferson said that because he thought Judaism was a horrible religion, and he considered the Jewish God and the Christian God to be totally different. Look at page 1437 of *Thomas Jefferson / Writings*, edited by Merrill D. Peterson, where Jefferson says in a letter to a friend that the God of the Jews is "a being of terrific character, cruel, vindictive, capricious and unjust," and then says "Jesus, taking for his type the best qualities of the human head and heart, wisdom, justice, goodness, and adding to them power, ascribed all of these, but in infinite perfection, to the Supreme Being, and formed him really worthy of their adoration." Later in the same letter, Jefferson writes that Moses "instilled into his people the most anti-social spirit towards other nations," while Jesus "preached philanthropy and universal charity and benevolence."

Item 26: Dawkins and the Tax Code

On pages 32-33 of *The God Delusion*, (page 53 of the paperback), Dawkins complains about preachers in the United States getting money "tax-free." Dawkins is lying. Clergymen in the United States pay taxes on their incomes just like everyone else. Clergymen don't have to pay Social Security taxes if they don't want to, but few of them take advantage of that rule, because if they did, they wouldn't be allowed to draw Social Security benefits in their old age.

It is true that in the United States one can get a tax deduction for donating money to a church, but there is no reason for Dawkins to be upset about that, because one can get a tax deduction for donating money to an atheist group too. Similarly, if a congregation gives its clergyman a rent-free house to live in, that is not counted as taxable income, but the same would be true if an atheist group gave its leader a rent-free house to live in, as long as the leader was serving the group in a way similar to the way a clergyman serves a congregation.

Item 27: Dawkins Lies About John Adams

On page 43 of *The God Delusion*, (page 65 in the paperback) Dawkins claims John Adams made some very anti-Christian statements. Once again, Dawkins fails to say what his source of information for these quotes is. Once again, Dawkins wants us to take his statements on faith. I suspect those quotes are phony, because we know for certain that Adams said in a letter to Jefferson in 1817, "Without religion, this world would be something not fit to be mentioned in public company – I mean hell." (Endnote 54.) We know Adams was a churchgoer, we know he was dismayed by the unorthodoxy of Thomas Jefferson's religious views, and we know that after his wife Abigail died, he wrote to Jefferson, "I believe in God and in his wisdom and benevolence, and I cannot conceive that such a Being could make such a species as the human merely to live and die on this earth. If I did not believe in a future state, I should believe in no God." For those facts, see, respectively, pages 391, 113, and 625 of the book *John Adams* by the famous historian David McCullough. If Dawkins had wanted to know the truth about Adams's religious beliefs, he could've looked at the index of that book and found the page numbers where Adams's religious beliefs are discussed. That's what I did. It took only a few minutes. But learning the truth was not Dawkins's goal. His goal was to deceive his readers.

Item 28: Theodicy

On page 64 of *The God Delusion*, (page 89 of the paperback), Dawkins asks why God allowed the Holocaust to happen. One wonders why he doesn't ask an Orthodox rabbi. Did that never occur to him?

Dawkins never considers the traditional Christian explanation: that all people are sinners, and therefore all of us deserve to be punished. Even small children deserve to have bad things happen to them, because if they lived long enough, they would inevitably become sinners just like everybody else. Because of our sins, we deserve to live in a world full of randomness, and because of this randomness, some people will suffer more than others, but Christ is our light and our comforter, and if we remember how He suffered, though He was completely sinless, and remember His promises to those who are faithful to Him, we will find the strength to carry our burdens.

An anecdote about St. John of the Cross, a sixteenth century Spanish monk, illustrates the point. One day he was preparing to go on a journey with another monk. Bandits were common on the roads in those days, and the other monk asked, if we are attacked by bandits, may we defend ourselves? St. John said absolutely not: when you become a clergyman, you give up the right to use violence in self-defense. No matter what happens, he said, we should just accept it as the punishment we deserve for our sins.

Of course, this leads to the question of whether faith in God really does give us the strength to carry our burdens. Primo Levi, an atheist who survived Auschwitz, said it did. "The believers lived better" he wrote, in moments of crisis and also "in the grind of everyday life" in Auschwitz. He goes on to say, "It was completely unimportant what their religious or political faith might be. Catholic or Reformed priests, rabbis of the various orthodoxies, militant Zionists, naïve or sophisticated Marxists, and Jehovah's Witnesses – all held in common the saving force of their faith." They had a philosophical framework that explained Auschwitz to them. "It was a divine punishment or expiation, or votive offering, or the fruit of capitalist putrefaction. Sorrow, in them or around them, was decipherable and therefore did not overflow into despair." (Endnote 55.)

One might also look at the life of Kim Phuc Phan Thi, a lady who grew up in South Vietnam during the war. (You can read about her in Wikipedia.) One day a South Vietnamese Air Force airplane accidentally dumped a bunch of napalm on her. She has had to have quite a lot of surgery since that day, and the pain was terrible, but after years of anger and bitterness, she found Christ. You can read her story in her autobiography, *Fire Road: The Napalm Girl's Journey Through the Horrors of War to Faith, Forgiveness and Peace*.

One can also look at a book called *The Light Shines On in the Darkness: Transforming Suffering Through Faith*, by Robert Spitzer, or a book called *The Case for Faith* by Lee Strobel.

Of course, John Calvin and Martin Luther preached that God is inscrutable, that He predestines some people for Heaven and others for Hell, that He gives faith to some and not to others, and nobody knows why, and it is useless to ask. (Endnote 56.) The presence of evil in the world, to Calvin and Luther, did not matter, because they believed there is no such thing as free will, so people who are predestined for Heaven will believe in God despite all the evil in the world, and those who are predestined for Hell will not believe in God, no matter what arguments they hear.

Other religious groups, such as the Catholic church, the Anglican church, and the Jewish denominations, do not believe in predestination. Their philosophers might ask, if there was no evil in the world, what a strange world it would be! A lady could give birth, and then just walk away, leaving the baby on the ground, certain that nothing bad would happen to it. Under such conditions, people would just pursue shallow pleasures, and love would not exist. Each person would just be a self-sufficient individual, feeling no need for any kind of community. An atheist might ask why God cannot make people love each other even though they do not need each other, but the answer is that if God is forcing people to love each other, then they are no longer free. Basically, the atheist is saying God should force people to become robots who will love each other because they are not capable of doing anything else. One can say that would be a good world only if one thinks freedom is bad.

It is surprising that Dawkins apparently has never thought of any of this.

Item 29: Dawkins Tries to be Logical

On page 78 of *The God Delusion*, (page 101 of the paperback) Dawkins argues that omnipotence and omniscience are incompatible, that if God knows what is going to happen, that means He doesn't have the power to change His mind.

The argument is based on a silly premise. Why would God want to change His mind? He already has all the information, He already has considered all the relevant factors, and therefore He always reaches the right decision the first time. Even if He answers prayers, that is only because he knew in advance that the person would pray for help.

Item 30: Dawkins and the First Mover

On pages 77-78 of *The God Delusion*, (pages 101-102 of the paperback) Dawkins discusses the argument that God must exist because there has to be a First Mover, somebody who got the universe started. Dawkins argues that the First Mover might be a natural process, not a supernatural being.

The problem with Dawkins's argument is that if matter, all the stuff in the universe, has always existed, that is truly difficult to imagine. How could it have always existed, without any person or process making it? How can it be an effect without a cause? It just doesn't make sense, unless one thinks matter itself is somehow supernatural. Trillions of years ago, quadrillions of years ago, quintillions of years ago, and on and on forever backward, it was there. How could that be? But if it used to not exist, and now does, as proponents of the Big Bang Theory believe, what caused it to come into existence? Some law of physics would have to exist that causes matter to be created out of nothing, but then of course, one has to wonder where that law of physics came from. Did it always exist? If so, that too is hard to imagine. Forever backward in time, that law of physics was always there, unmade by anyone? How could that happen? Why would there be a law of physics that has always existed? That idea seems no less supernatural than believing in God. It just doesn't seem possible that a natural object or process could be a First Mover.

In 2012, a physicist named Lawrence Krauss wrote a book called the *A Universe from Nothing: Why There is Something Rather than Nothing*. Krauss asked Dawkins to write an afterword for the book, so on page 189 of that book, Dawkins says Krauss has explained that "Not only does physics tell us how something could have come from nothing, it goes further, by Krauss's account, and shows us that nothingness is unstable; something was almost bound to spring into existence from it." Then on page 191, Dawkins says,

"Even the last remaining trump card of the theologian, 'Why is there something rather than nothing?' shrivels up before your eyes as you read these pages. If *On the Origin of Species* was biology's deadliest blow to supernaturalism, we may come to see *A Universe from Nothing* as the equivalent from cosmology. The title means exactly what it says. And what it says is devastating."

Unfortunately for Dawkins, those words are just not true. A philosophy professor named David Albert, who also has a doctoral degree in physics, wrote a review of Krauss's book for the *New York Times Book Review*, (see the March 25, 2012 issue) and demonstrated how wrong the book is. What the book actually says is that the universe sprang into being, not from nothing, but from the fundamental principles of quantum mechanics, and the book says absolutely nothing about where the fundamental principles of quantum mechanics came from. Albert also points out that even if we could prove that the fundamental principles of quantum mechanics came from some deeper law of nature, we would be left with the question of where that deeper law of nature came from. It too would have to have sprung from some even deeper law of nature, and so on. Therefore, it is obvious to anyone who thinks about it, that there is no logical way the universe could have emerged from nothing. Either there is some basic stuff in the universe that has always existed, and we don't know why it exists, or else all the matter in the universe came into existence because of a basic law of nature, and we don't know why that law exists. The title, *A Universe from Nothing*, is simply not true.

Currently, Albert wrote, physicists believe the universe is made of "relativistic quantum fields." These relativistic quantum fields, when arranged in certain ways, produce matter. But every honest physicist admits that nobody knows where the relativistic quantum fields come from, or why they exist at all.

It is clear that Dawkins shot his mouth off about a subject he knew nothing about. Tacitly, he has admitted it. *The New York Times Book Review* is always willing to print letters from authors who think their books have been misunderstood by reviewers, but neither Krauss nor Dawkins sent in a letter to try to prove Albert was wrong. They knew Albert had demolished their arguments.

A chap named Massimo Pigliucci has a blog called rationallyspeaking.blogspot.com. In his April 25, 2012 entry, he reports that in a recent interview, Krauss admitted that the title of his book, *A Universe from Nothing*, was dishonest, and said he gave the book that title so readers would be more "attracted to it." In other words, Krauss thinks it is okay to lie to his readers if that will help him sell more books. Pigliucci then points out the obvious fact that Krauss ought to be ashamed of himself for trying to deceive his readers that way.

As if in answer to Krauss and Dawkins, a science writer named Jim Holt published a book a few months later called *Why Does the World Exist? An Existential Detective Story*. One of the experts who is interviewed in that book is Steven Weinberg, a Nobel prize-winning physicist. Weinberg agrees with David Albert. He says too many people fail to notice that even if the laws of physics caused all the matter in the universe to suddenly erupt into existence billions of years ago, we are still left wondering where the laws of physics came from, and why they are the way they are. (Endnote 57.)

Item 31: Bertrand Russell

In a footnote on page 82 of *The God Delusion*, (page 106 of the paperback) Dawkins calls Bertrand Russell, a prominent British atheist, a "great philosopher."

The truth is that Bertrand Russell was a nitwit. In 1936, he wrote a book called *Which Way to Peace?* in which he said that modern war was so horrible that if Hitler declared war on Britain and France, Britain and France should just surrender and let Hitler take over. (Endnote 58.) As late as March 1939, Russell publicly declared that if Hitler attacked France and Britain, the United States should remain neutral and do nothing to help the French and the British. (Endnote 59.) Not until the war started did he reluctantly decide that Hitler had to be stopped. And this was not an isolated incident. During World War One, Russell sang the same song. He wanted Britain to be neutral, to just stand on the sidelines and let the Germans destroy democracy in France and Belgium. (Endnote 60.)

Can you imagine what Dawkins would say if some pope had said things like that? He would never stop complaining about it. But when an atheist says such things, Dawkins calls him a "great philosopher."

Item 32: Art

On pages 86-87 of *The God Delusion*, (page 111 of the paperback) Dawkins claims that Bach, Michelangelo, and other great artists could've been inspired just as much by science as by religion. Oh really? Why then has science not inspired any great art in the twentieth or twenty-first century? What great art was ever inspired by the theory of evolution or by quantum mechanics or by any other scientific principle? After all, because of population growth, there are more artists alive now than there were hundreds of years ago. Dawkins mentions no such art. Surely he would if there was any.

The greatest song in the history of rock music is called "Stairway to Heaven," not "Stairway of Evolution."

As near as I can tell, modern artists mostly seem to be afraid of science. Rightly or wrongly, they seem to associate science mostly with nuclear bombs, mind control, government surveillance technology, thalidomide, pesticides that kill birds, contaminated drinking water, and weird genetic experiments. You can see that in the opera, "Einstein on the Beach." It depicts Einstein as the father of nuclear weapons. You can see it in that Will Smith movie, *I, Robot*, where robots try to take over the world. You can also see it in Edward Albee's famous play *Who's Afraid of Virginia Woolf?* in which one of the characters rants about how, in his opinion, biologists are all a bunch of eugenicists.

Item 33: Shakespeare

On page 87 of *The God Delusion* (page 111 of the paperback) Dawkins says if Shakespeare had had to "work on commissions from the Church" *Hamlet*, *Macbeth*, and *King Lear* would never have been written.

What kind of weird criticism is that? If Shakespeare had had to work on commissions from the Harvard physics department, those plays would also not have been written, because subsidizing literary efforts is not what the Harvard physics department does. Similarly, subsidizing literature is not the church's job. Jesus said, "Go forth and make disciples of all nations." He didn't say, "Go forth and hand out money to writers."

Maybe what Dawkins is trying to say is that he thinks somehow the Christian churches are the enemy of literature, but if that is his point, he still isn't making sense. There is nothing unchristian about *Hamlet*, *Macbeth* and *King Lear*. Hamlet spends a great deal of time worrying about his soul, and in *Macbeth*, Prince Malcolm's mother is praised for her piety while the evil King Macbeth is portrayed as being in league with Satan. The Catholic Church didn't stop Cervantes from writing his great novel, *Don Quixote*, nor did it censor the novel after it was written, so why would it have stopped Shakespeare?

Item 34: The Events at Fatima

On pages 91-92 of *The God Delusion*, (pages 116-117 of the paperback) Dawkins discusses the mysterious events at Fatima, Portugal, in 1917. Three peasant children there claimed they saw the Virgin Mary on several occasions, at a particular location out in the countryside. Finally they said that Mary told them that at noon on October 13, 1917, a miracle would occur. Seventy thousand people gathered at that location on that day to see if there would be a miracle, and something strange did indeed happen. Those in attendance say they saw the sun "dance" in the sky, moving around in a zigzag pattern, emitting beams of light of different colors. Then, for a few seconds, it seemed to be plunging toward Earth. The crowd screamed in terror. Then the sun resumed its normal place in the sky. Dawkins admits "It is not easy to explain how seventy thousand people could share the same hallucination," but he declares it is even harder to believe that the Earth was temporarily ripped out of its orbit and nearly thrown into the sun "with nobody outside Fatima noticing."

That is a strange, strange statement. When I first heard about Fatima years ago, I took it for granted that the Earth was not really "temporarily ripped out of its orbit." I took it for granted that the miracle was that God simultaneously made seventy thousand people think they were seeing the sun dance, change colors, and then get drastically closer to the Earth. Dawkins never even considers that possibility. Is he really that unimaginative?

So, Dawkins never suggests a natural explanation for what happened at Fatima. Obviously, he can't think of one. This is not surprising. Atheists constantly tell us that miracles never occur, and if you say "What about Fatima?" they just walk away and refuse to talk about it. I guess one should give Dawkins credit for at least mentioning the subject. Carl Sagan wrote book after book, but he never said a word about Fatima. Obviously he was embarrassed that he couldn't think of a natural explanation for it.

Some atheists have argued that if you stare at the sun long enough, the sun will start to look like it is changing colors and dancing around in the sky. (How do they know this? Did these militant atheists actually stare at the sun for an hour to see what would happen?) I don't know whether that is true or not, and I'm not going to try it myself, because I don't want to hurt my eyes, but even if it is true, the fact is that nobody at Fatima was staring at the sun, because the three children did not predict that the miracle would have anything to do with the sun. The crowd was looking at the three children, who were kneeling in prayer.

Item 35: Who Wrote the Gospels?

On page 96 of *The God Delusion*, (page 122 of the paperback) Dawkins says the authors of the four gospels "almost certainly never met Jesus personally." He never explains why he thinks so. He wants us to just take that statement on faith. One can only laugh at such talk. It happened so long ago, how can anyone possibly say such a thing with confidence?

An Oxford University professor named Robin Lane Fox is considered an expert on ancient literature, and a few years ago he wrote a book about the Bible called *The Unauthorized Version*. He isn't religious, but he writes in that book that in his opinion, the Gospel of John was probably written by one of Jesus's disciples, an eyewitness to many of the events of Jesus's life. (Endnote 61.)

Item 36: Sir Isaac Newton

On page 98 of *The God Delusion*, (page 124 of the paperback) Dawkins says Sir Isaac Newton "did indeed claim to be religious." He makes it sound as though there is some doubt among historians about whether he really was. There isn't. Any scholarly biography of Newton will tell you that Newton spent so much time writing on religious subjects that his sincerity cannot be doubted. If he was a secret atheist who pretended to be religious just to avoid trouble, he could've avoided trouble just by going to church every Sunday, and doing nothing more. He didn't have to also spend so much of his spare time studying the Bible and writing about theology.

Item 37: The Intellectual Elite

On page 100 of *The God Delusion*, (page 127 of the paperback) Dawkins says polls show that few top scientists and members of the "intellectual elite" believe in a personal God.

So what? I bet if you had taken a survey in the United States in 1932, you would've found that communists, on the average, had much higher IQs than non-communists. But the communists were wrong all the same. Some very smart guys named John C. Calhoun, James Madison, George Washington, Robert E. Lee, Roger Taney and Judah Benjamin thought it was okay to own slaves, but they were wrong too.

Let's take a look at what George Orwell had to say. As I have already said, Orwell's morals leave a lot to be desired, but he was a good journalist. Nobody seems to doubt that he was good at noticing the facts that were right in front of his eyes. He wrote, during World War Two, that Britain's intellectual class had been wrong repeatedly. Look at this:

> "The average intellectual of the Left believed, for instance, that the war was lost in 1940, that the Germans were bound to overrun Egypt in 1942, that the Japanese would never be driven out of the lands they had conquered, and that the Anglo-American bombing offensive was making no impression on Germany. He could believe these things because his hatred of the British ruling class forbade him to admit that British plans could succeed."

Orwell went on to say "I have heard it confidently stated, for instance, that the American troops had been brought to Europe not to fight the Germans but to crush an English revolution. One has to belong to the intelligentsia to believe things like that: no ordinary man could be such a fool." He also noticed how popular Stalin was among British intellectuals, and said, "the British intelligentsia, with few exceptions, have developed a nationalistic loyalty towards the USSR and are dishonestly uncritical of its policies." (Endnote 62.)

Or look at Einstein, the greatest scientific genius of the twentieth century. In the 1920s and early 1930s, when Germany was a free country, he advocated pacifism. He wanted Germany to disband its military, and if Stalin invaded Germany, he thought the Germans should just surrender. Believe it or not, he thought having a military was such a horrible thing that it would be better to let yourself be ruled by a bloodthirsty brute like Stalin, rather than spend a few bucks every year, have a military, and deter him. You can read about this on page 371 of the critically-acclaimed book, *Einstein: His Life and Universe*, by Walter Isaacson, or in any other scholarly biography of Einstein.

Einstein thought that way because he was a fool, because he was the perfect example of a brilliant scientist who has no common sense.

Of course, when Hitler took over in Germany, Einstein suddenly changed his mind and announced that the countries that border on Germany should strengthen their militaries in order to deter the Nazis, and should be willing to fight. But he could never bring himself to oppose Stalin nearly as much as he opposed Hitler.

Steven Pinker, a famous psychology professor at Harvard University, has made pretty much the same argument that I'm making here. He has described at length the remarkable story of how the liberal intellectuals who dominate the social science departments in American universities refused, for decades, to admit that there was any such thing as human nature, and especially refused to admit that there are extremely high rates of violence in primitive tribal societies. Instead, based on paltry evidence, they clung to the ridiculous notion that primitive tribes are full of wonderful peaceful people who were morally far superior to modern Americans. (Endnote 63.)

Pinker also shows how American liberal intellectuals, for decades, could not bear to face the fact that men and women, on the average, have significantly different personalities, because of their genes. (Endnote 64.)

In fact, on page 341 of his book, *The Blank Slate: The Modern Denial of Human Nature*, Pinker summarizes my point quite well: "Anyone familiar with academia knows that it breeds ideological cults that are prone to dogma and resistant to criticism."

Item 38: Dawkins and Liberalism

On page 102 of *The God Delusion*, (page 129 of the paperback) Dawkins claims religiosity "strongly" negatively correlates with political liberalism. His source of information for this claim is a poll taken by one of his buddies.

The prominent social scientists Robert Putnam and David Campbell, a few years ago, took a survey of political and religious attitudes and reported their findings on page 386 of their book *American Grace*. When asked "Should abortion be outlawed? Or allowed only in cases of rape, incest or when the mother's life is at risk?" 78 percent of the most religious quintile said yes to one or both questions, while only 18 percent of the least religious quintile did. When the question was "Do you oppose same-sex marriage?" 60 percent of the most religious said yes, while only 16 percent of the least religious did. On those two issues, we truly see a correlation between religiosity and conservatism.

On other issues, the picture is not so clear. When the question was whether the government should take steps to reduce income inequality, 61 percent of the most religious quintile said yes, while 73 percent of the least religious quintile did. When the question was "Should we spend less on foreign aid?" 47 percent of the most religious said yes, while 52 percent of the least religious did. (I suspect guys like Dawkins will be surprised by that.) When the question was "Should the United States take an active role in the world?" 70 percent of the most religious quintile said yes, while only 60 percent of the least religious did. (I bet that will surprise Dawkins too.) When the question was "Is keeping the country safe from terrorism more important than protecting civil liberties?" 74 percent of the most religious quintile said yes, while 54 percent of the least religious did. When the question was "Should the United States decrease the number of immigrants allowed into the country per year?" 46 percent of the most religious quintile said yes, while 44 percent of the least religious did. When the question was "Do you support the death penalty?" the most and least religious quintiles were the same: 68 percent said yes.

Now let me point out some other facts.

In 2013, the Supreme Court reviewed the case of a guy who was forced by police to provide a DNA sample when he was arrested on a minor charge. The DNA sample matched the DNA from a rape that occurred years earlier, so the guy was convicted of sexual assault. The guy argued that the DNA evidence should've been excluded, because forcing him to provide the sample was an unconstitutional search. One would think that nobody with even a speck of common sense would want to deny the police the right to use such a great tool for solving crimes, but four justices did indeed say that, and three of the four were liberals. Four of the five who upheld the conviction were conservatives.

(That case was called *Maryland v. King*. One can look it up in Wikipedia, or at any law school library.)

Is that the kind of liberalism that Dawkins loves so much?

Or look at a Supreme Court case from 1984 called *Massachusetts v. Sheppard*. A woman was found murdered in a vacant lot. The police suspected her boyfriend, Sheppard. Sheppard didn't own a car, but around the time of the murder he had borrowed a car from a friend, and police found bloodstains in the trunk. They got a search warrant and found the victim's wig and bloodstained clothing in Sheppard's home. But the judge had made some mistakes when he filled out the search warrant form, and Sheppard's lawyers argued that therefore the wig and bloodstained clothing should be excluded from evidence. Seven Supreme Court justices rejected Sheppard's lawyer's argument, but two voted to turn this vicious hoodlum loose just because a judge had made small mistakes in a search warrant, and those two were the two most liberal justices, William J. Brennan and Thurgood Marshall.

Does Dawkins think we should all love that kind of liberalism too?

And let's look back to 1992. A black rapper named Sister Souljah got some attention by saying in an interview with the *Washington Post*, "I mean, if black people kill black people every day, why not have a week and kill white people?" Bill Clinton, being a sane man, pointed out that that statement was nothing but barbarism and that one cannot help black Americans by encouraging them to commit murder. Jesse Jackson, a liberal if there ever was one, refused to criticize Sister Souljah and demanded that Clinton apologize to her. (Clinton never did. See page 411 of Clinton's autobiography.)

Does Dawkins like that kind of liberalism too?

Look at the stop-and-frisk policy that the New York City police have instituted in recent years. After it was instituted, violent crime in New York City dropped drastically, by 34 percent since 2002. The police themselves have no doubt that stop-and-frisk is the reason why. When the police are aggressive, the hoodlums worry more about getting caught and become more cautious. They leave their guns at home, for example, for fear of being caught carrying a concealed firearm, and of course, if the hoodlums aren't carrying guns, it is less likely that some trivial argument will escalate into deadly violence. But the liberals can't stand that. Never mind that stop-and-frisk is saving lives. They want it declared unconstitutional, because some of the people who are being stopped and frisked find the experience annoying. Is that the kind of liberalism that Dawkins loves so much? Why can't the liberals understand that gun control laws don't do any good unless you give the police the power to enforce them?

(You can read about the controversy over the stop-and-frisk policy in an article by Jeffrey Toobin in the May 27, 2013 issue of *New Yorker* magazine.)

Look at pages 110-116 of Steven Pinker's book, *The Better Angels of Our Nature*. Pinker is by no means a religious man, nor is he a conservative, but he admits that ideas spread by liberals and socialists in the 1960s and 1970s, such as "if it feels good, do it," and the notion that the establishment was morally rotten, contributed to the drastic increase in crime in the United States in those decades.

Let's look at page 49 of the November 11, 2013 issue of *New Yorker* magazine. An article by the famous journalist Nicholas Lemann says a liberal policy, started by the Carter administration, wouldn't let the CIA and other intelligence agencies share information about Osama bin Laden and his followers with the FBI, because liberals were afraid that the CIA and other intelligence agencies would spy on American citizens. Mary Jo White was the U.S. attorney for the southern district of New York at the time, and she says this policy was a big handicap in her fight against terrorism. The policy was finally abolished by the George W. Bush administration. Does Dawkins like that kind of liberalism too?

And how about this? After Michael Dukakis, during the 1988 campaign, bragged repeatedly about being a member of the ACLU, conservatives pointed out that the ACLU wanted to legalize child pornography. The ACLU admitted that was true. Their position was that manufacturing child pornography can be outlawed, but once it is manufactured, possession and sale of it must be legal, because in their opinion, that is a form of freedom of speech. (Endnote 65.) What this means is that if you go to some poor country where the police are always willing to accept bribes, you can bribe the police to look the other way while you make films of 8-year-old children being raped, and the ACLU, if it ever got its way, would let you make big money by selling those films in the United States.

Is that also the kind of liberalism that Dawkins loves so much?

And look at this fact. To me, it is obvious that the biggest problem the human race faced in the twentieth century was Hitler, and in Great Britain, the liberals and socialists completely failed to understand that it was necessary to stand up to him. Instead, they babbled about how horrible war would be, and advocated appeasement. The conservatives in Britain did too, for a while, but in April 1939, Prime Minister

Neville Chamberlain and his Conservative Party finally woke up, decided Britain needed to beef up its military, and proposed a military draft. They had an overwhelming majority in the House of Commons, so their bills passed easily, but the liberals and socialists all voted no. (Endnote 66.) The liberals and socialists thought Hitler was bluffing and there would be no war, so they thought there was no need to strengthen the army. If they had been in command, the British would've been woefully unprepared when the war started, and Hitler would've won.

Is that also the kind of liberalism that Dawkins loves so much?

George Orwell made a similar point in 1940 in his famous essay, "The Lion and the Unicorn." Left-wing intellectuals had for the last twenty years been been praising hedonism and ridiculing courage and patriotism, he said, but the simple fact is that a nation of hedonists cannot possibly defeat the Nazis. (Endnote 67.) In 1941, Orwell said it even more bluntly: if the "left-wing intellectuals" had been more successful in influencing public opinion, the Nazis would be occupying London right now. (Endnote 68.)

But don't hold your breath waiting for Dawkins to talk about that. He'll rant all day about the need to "face the facts" about evolution, but he isn't going to face the facts about the history of British liberalism and socialism.

And if you really want to hear something weird, listen to this. For years, the gay and lesbian activists in the United States refused to do anything to win the right for gays and lesbians to serve in the military, because they were a bunch of pacifists and they hated the military. They didn't want anybody to serve in it, so winning the right for gays and lesbians to serve in it was the opposite of what they stood for. The people who ran the National Lesbian Conference in 1991 refused to even let a military lesbian give a speech at the conference. So strong was their hostility toward all things military that they wouldn't even listen to her. (Endnote 69.)

It is important to remember this fact, because I'm sure a few decades from now, people will find it astonishing that gay and lesbian organizations once had such an idiotic attitude.

And last but not least, Dawkins himself really doesn't seem to be all that liberal. He opposes affirmative action. (Endnote 70.) I wonder if he is aware of the fact that American liberals and socialists hold affirmative action to be almost sacred.

Item 39: Complexity

On pages 109 and 147 of *The God Delusion*, (pages 136 and 176 of the paperback) Dawkins makes a strange argument. He says it is silly to say "I can't imagine how the universe came to exist. There doesn't seem to be any way it could've happened naturally. A supernatural being must've done it," because, he claims, such a supernatural being would have to be at least as complex as the universe, and therefore we would be left with the question of how that supernatural being came to exist.

Without realizing it, he seems to be arguing that if we can't explain how a thing came to exist, then we shouldn't believe that it exists. That line of reasoning makes no sense at all.

He apparently can't see that to call a being "supernatural" is just a fancy way of saying "We don't understand that being. That being cannot be comprehended by the human mind."

He apparently can't see that if there is no natural, logical explanation for the existence of the universe, then a supernatural explanation, an illogical explanation, must be true, even if we don't understand it.

You don't have to take my word for it. A prominent science journalist named H. Allen Orr reviewed Dawkins's book in the January 11, 2007, issue of the *New York Review of Books* and said the same thing: Dawkins's argument on this point makes no sense. If God exists, then God exists, even if people don't understand Him and don't know why He exists, Orr said. After all, the laws of physics exist, even though we don't know why they exist or understand why they are the way they are.

Item 40: Knowledge

On page 126 of *The God Delusion*, (page 152 of the paperback) Dawkins complains that "religion ... teaches us that it is a virtue to be satisfied with not understanding." Dawkins is lying. The Bible says no such thing. But it does say morality is more important than knowledge, and it is right to say that. Before science was invented, life was hard, often short, and often extremely painful, but at least there were no nuclear bombs that could destroy all life on Earth, and no genetic engineers who could create viruses that could wipe out the human race. But Dawkins is not interested in addressing that concern.

(As I said earlier in this book, if you want proof that our knowledge of biochemistry and genetics is a problem, see the essay by the famous British physicist Martin Rees on pages 12-13 of the book, *What Should We Be Worried About?* edited by John Brockman. Rees says he is worried that "synthetic biology" technology will increase the danger of biological terrorism. It seems possible that soon, even people who aren't well educated will be able to create new viruses, using equipment that isn't terribly expensive.)

Item 41: Saint Augustine

On pages 132-133 of *The God Delusion*, (page 159 of the paperback) Dawkins claims St. Augustine once wrote, "There is another form of temptation, even more fraught with danger. This is the disease of curiosity. It is this which drives us to try and discover the secrets of nature, those secrets that are beyond our understanding, which can avail us nothing and which man should not wish to learn."

Dawkins says he found that quote in a book called *The Closing of the Western Mind* by Charles Freeman. (Why is it, I wonder, that Dawkins is willing to tell us his source for this quote, but not his sources for statements that he claims were made by Adams, Franklin, and Jefferson? Can it be because he got those other quotes from some crackpot website and he is ashamed to admit it?) So I checked that book and found that quote on page vii, and found that Dawkins misquoted it: Freeman has an ellipsis after the word "curiosity," where Dawkins puts a period. One has to wonder what words were left out. Furthermore, Freeman doesn't say where he found this quote. Why should we believe it is authentic when Freeman refuses to say where he found it? Obviously, we shouldn't.

Apparently Dawkins was willing to take what Freeman said on faith. Why take Charles Freeman on faith but not Jesus Christ?

Because I can't look up the place where Freeman found that quote, I don't know the context in which St. Augustine was speaking. I find it unlikely that St. Augustine opposed efforts to find out how to cure diseases and increase crop yields, for example. In all probability, he was merely saying that it is a waste of time to engage in the kind of abstract philosophizing that Plato and others enjoyed so much. Or else the quote is simply phony.

Item 42: The Origin of Life

An atheist has to believe that life started when a bunch of molecules somehow came together in just the right configuration to create a living organism. The molecules all just snapped together, like a toy made of a million Legos, and suddenly, they formed a living thing, something that could absorb energy from the surrounding environment and reproduce itself. After that, the atheists say, evolution took over, and that is why we are all here today.

On page 138 of *The God Delusion*, (page 166 of the paperback), Dawkins admits that a bunch of molecules all floating together in some pond or tide pool in just the right configuration to create a living organism is an extremely unlikely event, but he says with all the planets in the universe, and all the billions of years since the Big Bang, it was bound to happen at least once.

Well, I don't know about that. We often hear people say that anything is possible, but really, some things are impossible. A famous British astrophysicist named Sir Fred Hoyle used to say that the idea that a bunch of molecules could all float together into just the right configuration to suddenly form a living organism was no more likely than a tornado roaring through a junkyard and thereby building a jet airplane by slamming pieces of metal together. That's a good example. Even if you have a trillion planets and a trillion years, nature will never create a jet airplane. It simply isn't possible. A jet airplane requires intelligent design.

So how many molecules are we talking about, when we talk about the first living organism? How many would have to all float together and form the right configuration to create a very simple living organism? A hundred? A million? A billion? Dawkins doesn't say. Perhaps no biologist has ever tried to figure that out. That's the question we have to answer. If the answer is just a hundred, then it could happen. But what if it is a billion? And in exactly the right configuration? Then I'm not so sure. A billion is an awfully big number.

Iris Fry, a professor of the history of science at Tel Aviv University, has written a book called *The Emergence of Life on Earth*, which examines this question. She says on pages 193-194 that no respectable biologist today believes life started when a bunch of molecules accidentally floated together in just the right configuration to form a simple organism. The odds against that happening are just too great. Somehow, some molecule or group of molecules must have catalyzed the formation of the first organism, she says, but nobody has a plausible theory of what that molecule or group of molecules could have been, though many scientists have pondered the question. Jack Szostak, a Nobel laureate, said pretty much the same thing in an essay on pages 65-66 of the June 2018 issue of *Scientific American* magazine: nobody so far has come up with a convincing theory of how life could have started without divine intervention.

Item 43: Eukaryotic Cells

On page 140 of *The God Delusion* (page 168 of the paperback), Dawkins says the evolution of eukaryotic cells and of consciousness may have been even more unlikely than the emergence of the first life form.

Indeed.

Item 44: The Search for Extraterrestrial Intelligence

On page 138 of *The God Delusion* (page 166 of the paperback) Dawkins says he thinks it is good to spend money on SETI, the search for extraterrestrial intelligence. (In case you've never heard of this, there are scientists who spend their time listening for radio signals sent by intelligent beings on other planets. Millions of dollars are spent on this every year, and so far, the scientists have heard nothing. All the money for this listening comes from private donations, but the SETI scientists would love to get government funding.)

Why on Earth does Dawkins think it is a good idea to spend money on SETI? He fails to explain. There is absolutely no reason to believe that SETI will ever benefit the human race in any way, because there is no chance we would be able to understand any but the simplest message. The aliens could send us a picture of themselves, but there is no way they could tell us something complicated, such as how to cure cancer or cure lupus or solve our global warming problem. Even Carl Sagan, who was fanatically devoted to SETI, never explained how an alien message could be translated into English. Obviously he had no idea of how that could be done. Dawkins apparently has no idea either. So wouldn't it be better to spend the SETI money on fighting poverty, disease, and global warming instead? Of course it would. By advocating spending money on SETI, Dawkins is openly proclaiming that he doesn't care about the needs of the human race. Then he wonders why people think atheists are amoral.

Item 45: Simplicity

On page 155 of *The God Delusion* (page 184 of the paperback) Dawkins says the First Cause that got the universe started "must have been simple" and God can't be simple if he can talk to people and hear our prayers. But Dawkins doesn't explain why he thinks the First Cause must have been simple, and I don't see why we should assume that.

Item 46: A Complicated Process

On page 156 of *The God Delusion* (page 186 of the paperback) Dawkins says even if God exists, it is absolutely impossible that God "always existed" or "just popped into existence." If God exists, Dawkins says, He must be the end result of a complicated process. Maybe He evolved in a different universe, then created this one.

One reads that and wonders if Dawkins suffers from a severe neurosis. We don't know how the universe began, so how can Dawkins be certain that it wasn't created by a God who always existed or just popped into existence? Why is that inconceivable? If we believe that the supernatural is possible, then it is definitely conceivable. But if we, like Dawkins, just plain think the supernatural is impossible, then there is no point in talking further about the subject at all. Basically, Dawkins is saying, "The supernatural is impossible, but if it exists anyway, here are the rules it would have to follow." He doesn't see that if miracles are possible, then there are no rules that they have to follow. Miracles, by definition, are events that violate the rules of nature. Why can't Dawkins see that?

Item 47: Law and Order

On page 156 of *The God Delusion* (page 186 of the paperback) Dawkins says that "when I lived in America in the late 1960s, 'law and order' was politicians' code for anti-black prejudice."

Again, Dawkins is failing to face reality. The crime rate rose drastically in the United States in the 1960s (see the graph on page 92 of Steven Pinker's book *The Better Angels of Our Nature*, or look at the crime statistics in the back issues of a book called *The Statistical Abstract of the United States*, which the federal government publishes every year) but liberals such as Dawkins think we should have shrugged that off as no big deal. The people who were worried about crime were simply evil racists, in his opinion. The truth, of course, is that to be afraid of violent crime is a perfectly normal human feeling.

A black leftist named Eldridge Cleaver wrote a book called *Soul on Ice* that was published in 1968. In it, he declared that he had raped many white women over the years, and thought raping white women was a heroic, revolutionary act. Left-wing intellectuals had nothing but praise for that book. (You can read about this on page 114 of Steven Pinker's book, *The Better Angels of Our Nature*.) Does Dawkins find it strange that some white people found this rather frightening?

Item 48: Improbable

On page 158 of *The God Delusion* (page 188 of the paperback) Dawkins says that when we discuss the origin of the universe, we should ignore the possibility that a supernatural being created it, because, "The whole problem we started out with was the problem of explaining statistical improbability. It is obviously no solution to postulate something even more improbable."

One wonders why he is making this so complicated. Obviously, when we wonder why the universe exists, we first look for natural explanations. If we can't find one, we say "Maybe a supernatural being made the universe." That is all one can logically say. That is the end of the discussion. There is obviously no way to estimate the statistical probability or improbability that God exists. Why can't Dawkins see that?

Anyone can see what is going on here. Dawkins knows that the question of why the universe exists is a big question that atheism can't answer, so he has given up all hope of answering it and is instead hoping that if he just bangs his fist on the table often enough and shouts loudly enough, people will get the false impression that he has actually made a logical argument.

The only honest statement Dawkins could make on this subject is, "I just have a gut feeling that there is no god." But if he said that, a religious person could reply, "Well, I have a gut feeling that there is, and I have just as much right to my gut feelings as you do to yours." Dawkins would have no answer to that.

Item 49: The Peacock's Tail

On page 163 of *The God Delusion* (page 191 of the paperback) Dawkins admits that the peacock's tail does not help the peacock survive. That's a problem for Dawkins, because evolution is supposed to create efficient plants and animals that have only the characteristics that they need to survive and reproduce abundantly. Then Dawkins says the peacock's tail serves a purpose by attracting females. Why don't male birds of all bird species have big colorful tails then? He doesn't say. Apparently that question has never occurred to him. And wouldn't it be more efficient for evolution to give peahens the tendency to be attracted by something that actually helps the peacock survive? Dawkins never discusses that objection either.

I heard years ago, I think on one of those nature shows on PBS, that Darwin argued that peacocks evolved to have big tails because peahens preferred peacocks with big tails, so peacocks with big tails were more likely to find a mate than peacocks with short tails, and therefore, little by little, over the years, peacocks' tails became longer and longer. But the show also said that Darwin's friend and fellow biologist, Alfred Russel Wallace, responded to this by telling Darwin that he found it impossible to believe that a peahen would even notice that one peacock has a tail an eighth of an inch longer than another peacock's tail. Despite Wallace's objection, Darwin did not change his mind.

Item 50: Martin Luther

On page 190 of *The God Delusion* (page 221 of the paperback) Dawkins quotes some stupid statements that he says were made by Martin Luther. His source of information is a website. Doesn't he know the Internet is full of lies? Is he really that ignorant? Of course, I imagine one can trust the websites of reputable news organizations. If the website of the *Los Angeles Times* says Zadfrack Fiddlesticks has been convicted of shoplifting a can of beans, it's probably true. Wikipedia used to have lots of phony information, especially about controversial topics, but I've heard that the people who run Wikipedia have been cracking down on that. And I guess one can trust the websites of major universities to tell the truth about what's going on at the university. But why on Earth would one want to get information about Martin Luther from a website? If I wanted information about Martin Luther, I would go to a university library and read books and articles about him that have been written by history professors.

The obvious explanation here is that Dawkins will quote any website that tells him what he wants to hear. He doesn't care whether or not it is telling the truth.

Item 51: Oscar Wilde

On page 191 of *The God Delusion* (page 222 of the paperback) Dawkins quotes Oscar Wilde saying something disparaging about religion. One wonders why Dawkins thinks Wilde's opinion is worth hearing. Wilde was a talented writer, but he was a shallow man who devoted his life to being witty rather than wise. Look at page 197 of the book *Oscar Wilde* by an Oxford literature professor named Richard Ellman and you will see that when Wilde visited the United States in 1882, he spent a night in Jefferson Davis's home and publicly said, "The principles for which Jefferson Davis and the South went to war cannot suffer defeat."

The principle for which they went to war was slavery. Did Wilde not notice that? Or did he just not care?

Item 52: Dawkins and Slavery

On page 169 of *The God Delusion*, (page 197 of the paperback) Dawkins declares that "black slaves in America were consoled by promises of another life, which blunted their dissatisfaction with this one and thereby benefited their owners."

Oh really, Mr. Dawkins? How do you know that? Is there any evidence to support that theory? Dawkins doesn't present even one speck of evidence to support this claim. He wants us to just take it on faith. I've never heard of any slave or ex-slave who said, "I thought about running away from the plantation, but I didn't, because I was afraid it would be a sin," or anything like that. But it is a fact that Nat Turner, the leader of the only significant slave revolt in American history, was a Christian preacher (endnote 71) and it is also a fact that Harriet Tubman, who led many runaway slaves to freedom, was a devout Christian. (Endnote 72.) But Dawkins doesn't mention those facts. His goal is to deceive his readers, not educate them.

Look at pages 338-346 of the critically-acclaimed book, *Bury the Chains: Prophets and Rebels in the Fight to Free an Empire's Slaves*, by Adam Hochschild. White Christian missionaries preached to black slaves in Jamaica in the 1820s and 1830s that everyone was equal in the eyes of God. And the slaves listened too: the missionaries were amazed at how devout the slaves were. Then a major slave revolt broke out in Jamaica in 1831, led by a slave named Samuel Sharpe who was a deacon in a Baptist church. The slaveowners blamed the missionaries for the revolt, so after the revolt was crushed, several missionaries were jailed and approximately twenty Baptist and Methodist chapels were burned down by angry whites.

Maybe Dawkins doesn't believe that white Christian missionaries inspired slave revolts, but the slaveowners themselves definitely believed it.

A white missionary named William Knibb left Jamaica after the revolt, went back to Great Britain, and barnstormed the country, giving lectures and calling for the abolition of slavery. He had a large impact, Hochschild writes. His audiences were shocked to hear about the sufferings of the slaves, and shocked to hear that slaveowners had burned down Baptist and Methodist chapels. Succumbing to public pressure, the British government abolished slavery shortly thereafter.

Yet Dawkins sits there and declares that Christianity "benefited" the slaveowners. Will he never tire of telling lies?

Item 53: Why Does Religion Exist?

In chapter 5 of *The God Delusion*, Dawkins wonders why religion exists. He thinks it is perfectly obvious that religion is phony, so he wonders why it benefits people to believe something that is phony.

The simplest answer is that religion exists because people like it. I can't speak for other times and places, but in the United States today, people like the idea that they will be re-united with their loved ones after death. Is Dawkins really so cold-hearted that he can't imagine people thinking that way? And of course, there is a certain amount of fear of Hell too, but I don't think that is a major factor, because when I look around America, it doesn't seem to me that America is a nation of worriers. If we were the kind of people who worried a lot, we wouldn't have such a huge national debt.

Also, some people are religious out of love for justice. On Judgment Day, the evildoers will get what they deserve, and the virtuous people will be rewarded. Many people like that idea.

And some people feel a great love for Jesus Christ, this man of tremendous virtue who was persecuted so cruelly. The story of his victory over the grave is very inspiring.

And of course, if you want to think about it in terms of evolution, Christianity encourages people to refrain from violence, and refraining from violence not only helps society, but helps the individual. If a man gets angry about being insulted, and pulls out a gun or a knife, he may be killed. Therefore a Christian is more likely to survive and reproduce. Don't forget that killing a man over an insult was once considered a perfectly normal thing to do. Andrew Jackson did it, in his duel with Charles Dickinson, and he was very nearly killed in the process. (Dickinson's bullet passed very close to Jackson's heart. You can read about this in any biography of Jackson.) The fact that the Christian clergy opposed dueling is common knowledge among historians. When Alexander Hamilton was on his deathbed, an

Episcopal bishop gave him a stern lecture against dueling. (Endnote 73.) But Dawkins never thinks of that.

Even Dawkins's friend Steven Pinker agrees with me about this. Pinker, by no means a religious man, writes on page 91 of his book, *The Better Angels of Our Nature* that a society in which people follow a religion that preaches forgiveness is going to have less violent crime than a society in which people follow the normal human desire for revenge.

Christianity also helps the individual by making it less likely that he or she will contract a venereal disease. It's amazing to look back and see how many famous people had syphilis: James Joyce, Vladimir Lenin, Oscar Wilde, Guy de Maupassant, Howard Hughes, Franz Schubert. Back before the whites arrived in North America, syphilis seems to have been very common among the Native Americans. The men on the Lewis and Clark expedition discovered, much to their dismay, that it was just about impossible to have sexual intercourse with Native American women without getting syphilis. (Endnote 74.) Such was reality in those days, in any society that had liberal sexual morality. But Dawkins never thinks of that either.

Of course, one must also consider that religion my help people by giving them consolation in times of stress. If you believe that someday in Heaven you will again see your 5-year-old daughter who died of measles, that may help you keep going in life, instead of falling into despair and killing yourself, or becoming an alcoholic. Dawkins concedes in chapter 5 that this may be a benefit to the human race, but then he declares that that just isn't a "big enough theory" to explain why religion exists. What does he mean by that? He doesn't say. It seems pretty big to me. One is left wondering if Dawkins is so egotistical and cold-hearted that he truly cannot imagine that the deaths of close friends and relatives would ever upset someone very much. Einstein once said that there was nobody on Earth whose death would bother him all that much, despite the fact that he had two children at the time, and his mother and sister were still alive. (Endnote 75.) Maybe Dawkins is that cold-hearted too.

As I said earlier, Primo Levi was an Italian Jew who survived Auschwitz. On page 146 of his book *The Drowned and the Saved*, he wrote that religious prisoners were more likely than the average prisoner to survive Auschwitz, because their faith made them less likely to fall into despair. (He also says communist zealots were more likely than the average guy to survive Auschwitz, because they took comfort from their strong belief that communism would rule the world someday, even if they wouldn't live to see it.) Apparently Dawkins has never read that book.

Dawkins also writes, on page 353 of *The God Delusion* (page 395 of the paperback) that he knows of no evidence that religious people are happier than atheists. Well, like I just said, Primo Levi found that in Auschwitz, religious people were happier than the average guy. Jim Holt, a well-regarded science journalist, reviewed *The God Delusion* in the October 22, 2006 *New York Times Book Review*, and in that review he said, "Surveys have shown that religious people live longer (probably because they have healthier lifestyles) and feel happier (perhaps owing to the social support they get from church)." They have a higher birthrate too, Holt said, which is a Darwinian advantage. Dawkins's friend Daniel Dennett also has said, on page 272 of his book *Breaking the Spell*, that the evidence indicates that churchgoers are happier and healthier than other people, and seem to live longer. But Dawkins is blind to all that evidence.

A few years after *The God Delusion* was published, some striking data were published on this point. For years, the National Opinion Research Center at the University of Chicago has been conducting something called the General Social Survey to keep track of social trends. The GSS looked at white adults, ages 30 through 49, and found that those who go to religious services more than once per week report being happier than those who go once per week, who in turn are happier than those who go once per month, who in turn are happier than those who go only a few times per year, who in turn are happier than those who go only once per year, who in turn are happier than those who never go. (Endnote 76.) Now, of course, that doesn't necessarily prove that religiosity causes happiness. Maybe cause and effect works the other way around. Maybe the people who never go to church are just cynical, negative people who believe in nothing and think the whole world is a swindle and who therefore are just chronically angry, or maybe they are egomaniacs who are chronically dissatisfied because the world refuses to give them the glory, laud and honor that they think they deserve. But still, when Dawkins says religious people aren't happier than atheists, he is wrong.

Item 54: Dawkins Misunderstands Cargo Cults

In the last few pages of chapter 5 of *The God Delusion*, Dawkins discusses cargo cults, odd little groups that have sprung up among the natives of the South Pacific. According to the experts, the story is this: during World War Two, American military personnel arrived in the south Pacific with their advanced technology, and their chocolate bars, canned hams, liquor and other foodstuffs that they sometimes shared with the natives. The natives were very impressed by this cornucopia, so after the war ended and the American military left, the natives yearned for more shipments of all that stuff, which they called "cargo." They developed the idea that if they acted like American military personnel, marching around, carrying wooden rifles, saluting the American flag, and so on, the cargo planes would return, making them all rich. So that is what some of them have done, for years.

Dawkins seems to be saying that early Christianity was like a cargo cult. What he fails to see is that if that is true, that undermines the atheist argument. The cargo cults are based on facts, not fantasy. The cargo was real. Ships really did arrive and deliver wonderful stuff. So if early Christianity was like a cargo cult, that means Jesus really did heal the sick and rise from the dead.

Item 55: Returning from the Dead

On page 206 of *The God Delusion* (page 239 of the paperback), Dawkins says there are "cults" around Elvis Presley and Princess Diana. What a barefaced lie. Those two are greatly beloved, but nobody worships them. Nobody, except maybe a deranged person here or there, believes they have risen from the dead. Dawkins is simply blowing smoke.

A theologian named William Lane Craig has pointed out what Dawkins is missing here. The simple fact is that in the Middle East, in the first century A.D., something very strange happened. A large number of people became convinced that a man, whom many of them had known personally, had risen from the dead. Never before in human history had a significant number of people become convinced of such a thing, and it has never happened again in all the years since. (Endnote 77.) One has to wonder why it happened that one time. One has to wonder if it happened because that man really did rise from the dead.

(Let me make myself clear. I know the ancient Greeks had myths about people going down to the land of the dead and then coming back to Earth. They believed that Orpheus did that, for example. But none of the ancient Greeks ever said they had actually met Orpheus. They had no personal knowledge. They just relied on old stories. The early Christians, on the other hand, really did say they had seen Jesus both before and after his resurrection. That is the crucial difference.)

Item 56: Hate Mail

On pages 211-214 of *The God Delusion* (page 242-245 of the paperback), Dawkins says he knows some atheists who claim they have received hate-mail. It never occurs to him that the angry anti-atheist letters that he quotes from might've been written by the atheists themselves so they can have the pleasure of falsely claiming that they are being opposed by a multitude of evil dimwits. Plenty of people over the years have falsely claimed to be the victims of hate speech or hate graffiti or hate crimes. If Dawkins doesn't believe that, he should go to the Proquest Newspaper Database and look up Crystal Magnum, Dayna Morales, Aimee Whitchurch, Alexandra Pennell, Tawana Brawley, Jeannine Risley, and Stacie Racaniello.

I've heard clergymen claim they get hate-mail too. What does that prove? Nothing, really. The police officer who killed Michael Brown in Ferguson, Missouri, says angry liberals have sent him plenty of hate mail, and some have even threatened to kill his daughter. (Endnote 78.) Does Dawkins think this proves that liberalism is rotten? When the famous conservative William F. Buckley ran for mayor of New York City, he received death threats too. (Endnote 79.) Does that prove liberalism is rotten?

Bengt Holst, the scientific director at the Copenhagen Zoo, has received death threats because he had a healthy young giraffe killed, simply because the zoo had too many giraffes, and then had it dissected in front of an audience of school children. (Endnote 80.) Does Dawkins think that proves that animal rights activists are rotten people?

After Charles Lindbergh became a prominent voice for keeping the United States out of World War Two, he received a great deal of hate mail from anti-Nazi people. Some even threatened to kill his children. (Endnote 81.) Does Dawkins think that means it was bad to be an anti-Nazi?

Item 57: Social Darwinism

In a footnote on page 215 of *The God Delusion* (page 246 of the paperback), Dawkins admits that teaching people about evolution can result in the spread of social Darwinism.

I'm not going to give Dawkins much credit for admitting this. It is so obvious that it would be weird if he didn't admit it.

Item 58: Maimonides

On page 254 of *The God Delusion* (pages 288-289 of the paperback), Dawkins quotes the famous Jewish rabbi Maimonides as saying, "If one slays a single Israelite, he transgresses a negative commandment, for Scripture says, Thou shalt not murder. If one murders willfully in the presence of witnesses, he is put to death by the sword. Needless to say, one is not put to death if he kills a heathen." Dawkins thinks this is an example of the awful kind of thinking that is encouraged by religion.

I have no idea of whether or not Dawkins is quoting Maimonides accurately, but let me just say that if he is, doesn't this nasty attitude explain why there was so much antisemitism hundreds of years ago? If this is what the greatest Judaist rabbis were teaching their people, doesn't that explain why many gentiles didn't want Judaists living among them? Doesn't that explain why Shakespeare, when he wrote *The Merchant of Venice*, took it for granted that Judaists were a bunch of scoundrels? Dawkins should admit that.

Item 59: Fear

On page 322 of *The God Delusion* (page 362 of the paperback) Dawkins says it is terrible that Christian preachers scare people by talking about Hell.

The history of the twentieth century is full of atheist mass murderers such as Hitler, Stalin, Mao, Pol Pot, Kim Il-Sung, Kim Jong-Il, Mengistu and Milosevic, who did what they did because they had no fear of Hell, yet Dawkins sits there and says it is bad to make people feel afraid of Hell.

And if Dawkins thinks it is awful to scare people by talking about Hell, one wonders why he hasn't noticed that many people think atheism is pretty depressing too. Obviously, it is much more cheerful to think that one will see one's dead friends again someday. So does Dawkins think it is bad for atheists to depress people by preaching that there is no afterlife?

Item 60: Temptation

On page 229 of *The God Delusion* (page 261 of the paperback) Dawkins wonders whether religious people really are more likely than "unbelievers" to resist temptation when they find themselves in a situation where they can get away with doing something rotten that would benefit them. It never occurs to him to conduct an experiment and find out.

A Harvard economist named Richard B. Freeman led a massive effort years ago to examine the lives of young black men in the ghetto, and found, among other things, that those who went to church were a lot less likely to commit crimes than those who didn't go to church. (Endnote 82.)

Two psychological researchers named Azim F. Shariff and Ara Norenzayan did an experiment a few years ago in which they divided people into three groups based on their answers to a questionnaire about their religious beliefs. The three groups were the atheists, the people who see God as a loving forgiver, and the people who see God as a strict judge. Then they gave the people a chance to cheat on a task and secretly observed them. The people who said they saw God as a strict judge were significantly less likely to cheat than the atheists and the people who saw God as a loving forgiver. (Endnote 83.)

That is pretty much what one would expect, isn't it?

Item 61: Callous and Selfish Hedonists

On page 227 of *The God Delusion* (page 259 of the paperback), Dawkins rants that one has to have a very low opinion of the human race to think that only belief in God prevents people from becoming "callous and selfish hedonists, with no kindness, no charity, no generosity."

The odd thing though is that he supports his argument by quoting a prominent atheist named Michael Shermer. Doesn't Dawkins know that Shermer is a libertarian, a man who wants to abolish Social Security and Medicare and food stamps and every other government program that helps the needy? Shermer really is a callous and selfish hedonist with "no charity, no generosity." In his book *The Science of Good and Evil*, Shermer declares on pages 239-240 that he is a follower of the libertarian philosopher Robert Nozick, who thought the government should do nothing but fight crime and enforce contracts, and that it was evil to force the rich and the middle class to pay taxes to help the needy. Dawkins quotes from Shermer's book. Is it possible that he never read pages 239-240 and doesn't know that Shermer is a callous libertarian? Or is Dawkins simply trying to cover up the truth?

Of course, as I have already said, the evidence presented on pages 445 through 465 of the book *American Grace* by Robert Putnam and David Campbell shows that atheists really are less generous than religious people. The religious people are even more likely to donate to secular charities than the atheists are, and are even more likely to donate blood. Dawkins may gnash his teeth when he hears that, but that is the way it is.

Dawkins also fails to discuss Einstein in this context. Dawkins admits Einstein was an atheist, but never mentions the fact, which I discussed earlier in this book, that Einstein was a murderer, with the morals of a hitman. If Einstein, a great genius, could conclude that it was logical to kill innocent people in cold blood just so he could make some money, doesn't that indicate to Dawkins that atheism might cause deterioration in the human race's moral standards?

Item 62: High-Crime States

On page 229 of *The God Delusion* (page 262 of the paperback) Dawkins cites some statistics, saying that the most politically conservative American states, which he assumes are also the most religious, have some of the highest crime rates.

That argument makes no sense at all. No sociology professor would take it seriously, because anyone can see that even if conservative states have high crime rates, that does not mean that the conservative people are the ones committing the crimes.

Dawkins fails to notice that these high-crime states to which he refers are the states with the highest percentages of blacks. The fact that blacks have a much higher crime rate than whites is well-known, but I doubt Dawkins or anyone else would claim religion is the reason for that. See, for example, a book called *Enough* by a black journalist named Juan Williams. Williams admits on page 116 that in 2004, the most recent year for which there was data at the time Williams wrote the book, blacks were 13 percent of the population of the United States but committed 51 percent of the murders.

The undeniable fact is that criminals tend to be liberals. Researchers who looked into this found that when American convicted felons are allowed to vote, they are much more likely to register as Democrats than as Republicans. That is why, in recent years, many liberals have been saying that we should let convicted felons vote. They know that will help their side win elections. That is why Terry McAuliffe, the Democratic governor of Virginia, suddenly restored voting rights to 13,000 convicted felons, just in time for the 2016 election. (Endnote 84.)

Dawkins also fails to mention that the states with the lowest murder rates also tend to be politically conservative. Dawkins published *The God Delusion* in 2006, so let's look at the data from the 2005 *World Almanac and Book of Facts*. If you look at all fifty states plus the District of Columbia, the lowest murder rate is in North Dakota: just 0.8 murders per year per 100,000 people in the population. North Dakota is also one of the most lopsidedly conservative states. George W. Bush got 197,000 votes there in 2004, versus 111,000 votes for John Kerry. The second-lowest murder rate is 0.9, in New Hampshire, which Kerry carried by a slim margin, 341,000 to 331,000. The third-lowest murder rate is 1.1, in Maine, which Kerry carried by 397,000 to 330,000. The fourth-lowest murder rate is 1.4, in South Dakota, which Bush carried by another lopsided margin, 233,000 to 149,000. The fifth-lowest through tenth-lowest are, in order, Iowa, Montana, Hawaii, Oregon, Utah and Vermont. Three of those went for Bush, three for Kerry. (Utah went for Bush by an amazingly lopsided margin: 664,000 to 221,000.) Meanwhile, the highest murder rate was 46.2, in the District of Columbia, which went for Kerry by 203,000 to 21,000. (And that is the highest murder rate by a large margin: the second-highest was 13.2, in Louisiana.)

If there is any pattern here, I think it shows that conservative places tend to be more peaceful than liberal places. Is it really possible that Dawkins didn't notice that? It is more likely that he noticed it, but just didn't want to mention it. He was trying to deceive his readers, not educate them.

Item 63: The Flood

On page 238 of *The God Delusion* (page 269 of the paperback) Dawkins says it is terrible that God killed so many people in Noah's flood.

The answer to that is that God gives life, and God has the right to take it away. It was nice of God to give you any life at all. You should thank him for that. He has no obligation to give you eighty years, or whatever you think a normal lifespan should be.

Dawkins also says it is terrible that so many animals died in Noah's flood. Apparently he forgets that every animal dies eventually anyway, and what difference does it really make if a dog lives only five years instead of fifteen? Logically, if you are going to complain about animals being killed, you have to be a vegetarian, but Dawkins never says he is. Apparently logic doesn't interest him.

Item 64: Lot's Daughters

On page 240 of *The God Delusion* (page 272 of the paperback) Dawkins talks about the story of Lot in the Book of Genesis. Dawkins thinks it is terrible that when an angry mob gathered outside Lot's house, and demanded that he hand over his houseguests to them for gang rape, Lot offered the mob his two daughters instead.

Let me stress, the Bible doesn't say it was good for Lot to do that. It only records that that is what he did.

I think it should be obvious that in a situation like that, there is no good answer, so one answer is just as good as another. I wouldn't do what Lot did in that situation, but in those days, the duty of protecting houseguests was taken a lot more seriously than it is today. It's like the well-known lifeboat scenario. If a bunch of people are stuck in a lifeboat, and the lifeboat is sinking because there are just too many people in it, who gets pushed overboard? I guess now days most Americans would say the eldest should be sacrificed, because it is tragic for the young to die when they have had so little chance to live, but Confucius taught that the youngest should be sacrificed in a situation like that, because if the youngest don't serve their elders, what incentive is there for people to have children and keep the human race going?

Dawkins thinks Lot's decision was motivated by sexism. Maybe it was. Like I said, the Bible doesn't say Lot was right. Or what if Lot just thought his houseguests seemed like better people than his daughters? What if he thought his daughters were stupid, selfish, and interested only in foolish pleasures? Dawkins fails to even consider this possibility.

Imagine this situation. Mr. X is fifty years old, captain of a spaceship. There are two other people in the ship with him: Shnerga, his twenty-five year old daughter, and Fred, a twenty-five year old crewman. Fred once ran into a burning building to rescue a baby. Shnerga has openly declared that she would never do something like that. "That's just dumb!" she sneered. An accident happens on board that destroys most of the oxygen supply, so now there is only enough oxygen for one person to get back to Earth alive. If Mr. X decides that Fred is just a better person than Shnerga, and decides he will kill her and then kill himself so Fred can live, would Dawkins criticize Mr. X for that? I doubt it. But it never occurs to him that Lot may have been in a similar situation.

Item 65: Dawkins on Similarities

On page 241 of *The God Delusion* (pages 273-274 of the paperback) Dawkins says the story of Gibeah (which is in the Bible, in the Book of Judges) is so similar to the story of Lot and his houseguests that he suspects the story of Gibeah is phony.

Why in the world does Dawkins find it hard to believe that similar events can happen hundreds of years apart? Look at American history. In 1945, a liberal president from the North died, and was succeeded by a vice president from a former slave state who proposed significant new civil rights legislation, got the United States involved in a war in East Asia, was elected president in his own right once, and was so unpopular by the end of his time in office that he chose to not seek re-election, even though he was eligible to do so. In 1963 and the years that followed, all of that happened again. I wonder, a thousand years from now, will some guy like Dawkins look back at that and claim it can't be true, that two such similar series of events couldn't have happened in so short a time? Or look at the fact that in 1960, the incumbent vice president of the United States was nominated for president by his party, and after performing badly in televised debates, lost an extremely close election to a man from a wealthy family. In 2000, that same thing happened again.

Item 66: Abraham and Isaac

In the Book of Genesis, God tests Abraham by commanding him to make a human sacrifice of his son Isaac. Abraham was willing to obey, but at the last second, God tells Abraham to stop, and praises Abraham for being so obedient. On page 242 of *The God Delusion* (page 275 of the paperback) Dawkins says this must've been a terrible trauma for Isaac.

Dawkins fails to remember that some people just don't get upset easily. We hear a lot about the soldiers who suffer from post-traumatic stress disorder, and I'm certainly not going to minimize the seriousness of that problem, but the simple fact is that many soldiers never suffer from it. Supreme Court Justice Oliver Wendell Holmes was wounded three times during the Civil War, and saw plenty of horrible things, but he seems to have shrugged it off without much difficulty. Ulysses Grant saw plenty of horrible things too, but he too seems to have not been terribly bothered by them.

Life was rough in the days of Abraham, and farmers and herdsmen are rarely sentimental about their animals. Isaac doubtless had seen many animals being killed and butchered, and he had probably seen people die too, from one thing or another. A guy gets kicked in the head by a horse or a mule or a camel, and suddenly he is dead. Isaac probably knew perfectly well that death can be sudden, that any day might be one's last. Once Abraham explained to Isaac that he was never in any danger, that God had intended all along to call off the sacrifice at the last minute, Isaac probably accepted that and didn't fret about it too much. Why does Dawkins assume that Isaac was such a fragile flower that he would be traumatized by this incident?

Item 67: Jephthah

On page 243 of *The God Delusion* (page 276 of the paperback) Dawkins complains about the story of Jephthah, a great Israelite military hero who goes out to battle and vows that if God gives him victory, he will sacrifice the first creature that comes out to greet him when he gets home. The first creature turns out to be his daughter, so Jephthah sacrifices her.

It is important to note that the Bible does not say this was a good thing for Jephthah to do. It only records that Jephthah did it. In fact, in the Old Testament, the prophets frequently stress that God does not want human sacrifices, that only wicked pagans do such things. (See chapter 18, verse 21 of the Book of Leviticus, and chapter 23, verse 10 of the Second Book of Kings, and chapter 16, verses 20-21 of the Book of Ezekiel.) Probably the story was included in the Bible only as a cautionary tale, the point being that one should not make rash vows.

It is common for Christians and Jews to give their children the names of heroes from the Bible, but I've never heard of any baby being given the name Jephthah. That tells us something. Neither Christians nor Jews ever considered him a role model.

Item 68: Jericho

On page 247 of *The God Delusion* (page 280 of the paperback) Dawkins complains about the Battle of Jericho, and other occasions when the Israelites slew their enemies without mercy.

Once again, all one can say is that God gives life, and God has the right to take it away. God had the right to tell the Israelites to do that.

Dawkins says the Battle of Jericho is "morally indistinguishable" from Hitler's invasion of Poland. Not true. Hitler never claimed God told him to invade Poland, and even if he had, no Christian would've found that claim plausible. A Christian believes that Jesus told us everything we need to know about morality, and nothing Jesus said could have been plausibly used by Nazi propagandists to justify the invasion of Poland.

But on the other hand, the famous agnostic journalist H.L. Mencken saw nothing wrong with Hitler's invasion of Poland. He said so in a letter to a friend. (Endnote 85.) But don't hold your breath waiting for Dawkins to talk about Mencken.

Item 69: Dawkins Is Too Cowardly to Answer a Tough Question

On page 249 of *The God Delusion*, (page 283 of the paperback) Dawkins quotes a scientist named Steven Weinberg as saying it is no surprise when good people do good things and when bad people do bad things, "But for good people to do evil things, it takes religion." But Dawkins never considers that religion might make some people behave better than they would otherwise. Apparently he considers that impossible, but he fails to say why. He presents no evidence. He wants his readers to just take it on faith.

Isn't it odd that Weinberg and Dawkins think religion can influence people to make them worse, but is powerless to make them better? Psychologically, how does that work? It's like saying there is a pair of shoes that can be used to walk east, but can't be used to walk west.

Item 70: Atheists and Vandalism

Also on page 249 of *The God Delusion*, (page 283 of the paperback) Dawkins talks about vandalism of ancient sites committed by Muslim militants, and declares "I do not believe there is an atheist in the world who would bulldoze Mecca."

To put it mildly, I find that statement very very wrong. There are billions of people on Earth. Does Dawkins really think that among all those people, there is not one single atheist who is a nasty person? After the atheists Hitler, Stalin, Mao, Pol Pot, Milosevic and Mengistu committed mass murder, after the murders committed by atheists and agnostics such as Lee Harvey Oswald, James Earl Ray, and Timothy McVeigh, Dawkins can't imagine an atheist committing vandalism? One feels astonished at how blind Dawkins is to the facts of history. Once again, one suspects Dawkins knows perfectly well that he is talking nonsense, but does it anyway, because he knows he can make money by telling his fans the lies they want to hear. "Tell more lies" is his motto.

There used to be a church in Russia called the Cathedral of Christ the Savior. It was the largest Orthodox church in the world. It was demolished in 1931 on orders from Stalin. (Endnote 86.) That proves right there that Dawkins is wrong.

And Dawkins is apparently unaware of the fact that during World War Two, when the Allies didn't bomb Rome very much because they didn't want to damage all the famous buildings and art treasures that were there, the atheist science fiction writer H.G. Wells was outraged by that decision. He wrote a newspaper article called "Why don't we bomb Rome?" in which he angrily charged that for no good reason, Catholics in the British government were preventing Rome from being bombed. (Endnote 87.)

Item 71: Family Life

On page 250 of *The God Delusion* (page 284 of the paperback) Dawkins criticizes Jesus because Jesus told people to leave their families and follow him.

Family life is a fine thing, but it should be obvious that some things are more important. Millions of immigrants came to America, left their families behind in Europe, and never saw them again. We call them heroes, because they built this country. If it was good for them to do that, just for money, why is it bad to leave your family, follow Jesus, and try to bring the Gospels to the human race? Or look at the slaves who ran away from their plantations and never saw their friends and relatives again. They thought freedom was worth it. If freedom was worth it, why is preaching the Gospel not worth it?

In the 1800s, a Belgian farm boy named Damien de Veuster left his family, became a Catholic priest, and became a missionary in Hawaii, taking care of lepers when nobody else would. (You can look him up in Wikipedia, or any good encyclopedia.) He was a great saint, and after he left Belgium, he never saw his parents again. Does Dawkins really think that was a bad thing for him to do?

Item 72: Original Sin

On page 251 of *The God Delusion* (page 285 of the paperback) Dawkins complains about the doctrine of original sin and asks "What kind of ethical philosophy is it that condemns every child, even before it is born, to inherit the sin of a remote ancestor?"

Original sin is just the idea that everyone who lives a normal lifespan will surely commit some sins. It is inevitable, because nobody is perfect. We all have a tendency to be selfish, and to disregard the needs of others. Even Dawkins's friend Edward O. Wilson has written that evolution has made people selfish, at least some of the time. (Endnote 88.) Steven Pinker, another one of Dawkins's friends, has admitted that it isn't normal for people to care as much about total strangers as they do about close friends and relatives. (Endnote 89.) Is that really so hard for Dawkins to understand? Does he really think there are sinless adults on Earth today? Of course there aren't, because everybody has original sin in their hearts.

Of course, maybe the explanation here is that Dawkins doesn't think severe selfishness is a sin. Maybe he thinks severe selfishness is normal, healthy behavior. Maybe that explains why he has been divorced twice.

Item 73: Morality

On page 252 of *The God Delusion* (page 286 of the paperback) Dawkins complains that "the Christian focus is overwhelmingly on sin sin sin sin sin sin sin."

It should be perfectly obvious that anyone who cares about morality is going to spend a lot of time thinking about sin. Morality is obviously the most important subject in all of human life, but Dawkins apparently dislikes thinking about it. We already saw that in Item 6, where Dawkins declared that murderers should not be punished, because punishing murderers is, in his opinion, just "vengeance."

Item 74: Dawkins Feels No Need for Evidence

On page 252 of *The God Delusion* (page 286 of the paperback) Dawkins approvingly quotes Sam Harris as saying the "principal concern" of the Christian clergy is sexual sin. Neither Dawkins nor Harris presents any evidence to support that claim. They want their readers to just take it on faith. In the churches I've attended over the last few decades, sexual sin has rarely been mentioned in the sermons. The most common themes, it seems to me, are urging people to be generous to the needy and urging people to forgive each other.

Item 75: Sacrifice

On page 253 of *The God Delusion* (page 287 of the paperback) Dawkins criticizes the whole idea of Christ's sacrifice on the cross, calling it "vicious, sado-masochistic, and repellant."

All one can say in response is no, it isn't. We all deserved to be punished eternally for our sins, but Christ, who was sinless and deserved no punishment whatever, volunteered to pay the penalty for us, just like a friend who pays your speeding ticket for you. What could be simpler? If Dawkins finds that theory implausible, all I can say is that we will find out on Judgment Day who is right.

Dawkins says God could've forgiven the sins of the human race without Jesus having to make his sacrifice on the cross. The traditional response of the Christian theologians to that objection is that justice requires that there be a penalty paid for sin, and because justice is a virtue, God, by His very nature, must pursue justice.

Besides, Jesus was God. If God chooses to inflict suffering on Himself, that is none of Dawkins's business. Why does he think he has the right to run someone else's life?

Item 76: Dawkins Ignores the Obvious

On pages 252-253 of *The God Delusion* (page 286 of the paperback) Dawkins talks about the so-called Gospel of Judas, an ancient book discovered by someone in Egypt several years ago. The Gospel of Judas says Judas betrayed Jesus only because Jesus asked him to, as part of the plan of redemption. Dawkins says this means it is terrible that Judas has gotten so much blame over the years.

Apparently the obvious truth never occurs to Dawkins: that the Gospel of Judas does not tell us what really happened. It was written more than a hundred years after Jesus was crucified, apparently by a member of a small sect that was considered strange even at the time. It is a bunch of nonsense, a phony gospel, and historians do not believe that it tells us the truth about Jesus and Judas. (Endnote 90.) I dare Dawkins to name even one history professor who believes the Gospel of Judas is an accurate account of what happened in Jesus's life. There are none.

Once again, we see that Dawkins believes any idiotic book or website, as long as it tells him what he wants to hear. He couldn't care less about the evidence, or about what the experts say.

For readers who don't know much about ancient literature, I can tell you that it was common knowledge among early Christian leaders that there were lots of phony gospels around, with names like the Gospel of Judas, the Gospel of Peter, the Gospel of Thomas and so on. There were phony letters ascribed to St. Paul too. In chapter 2, verse 2 of his Second Letter to the Thessalonians, St. Paul warns his readers that phony letters are being circulated that were allegedly written by him. But of course, because they were phony, the early Christian leaders rejected them when they were compiling the New Testament. There is nothing unusual about this. Phony documents are pretty common in human history. Back in the 1980s, someone claimed to have found Hitler's diary, but after much hullabaloo in the news media, that diary was proven to be phony. You can read about this episode in the book *Selling Hitler: The Story of the Hitler Diaries*, by Robert Harris. Back in the 1700s, a fellow in Scotland claimed he had found some ancient poems written by someone named Ossian. He published them in a book, and made a lot of money from that book, but it turned out to be a fraud. Literary experts today agree that the man who claimed to have found the Ossian poems actually wrote them himself. (You can read about this by looking up Ossian in Wikipedia or the *Encyclopaedia Britannica*.) The hoax led to a good joke though. The famous literary critic Samuel Johnson thought the Ossian poems were phony, so a friend said to him one day, "But Doctor Johnson, do you really think there are any men alive today who could write such poetry?" Johnson replied, "Yes, many men. And many women. And many children."

Item 77: Jesus and the Jews

On page 253 of *The God Delusion* (page 286 of the paperback) Dawkins says many Jews have been killed because of the "Christ-killer story."

Let's go over the facts. The Jews have a holy book called the Babylonian Talmud that was written a few hundred years after Jesus was born. (There is a similar but separate book called the Palestinian Talmud.) The Babylonian Talmud says the Jewish authorities killed Jesus for being a sorcerer and for claiming to be the son of God. The Babylonian Talmud also says Jesus deserved death, and is now in Hell. If you haven't got time to read the Babylonian Talmud, you can read about this subject in a short book called *Jesus in the Talmud* by Peter Schafer. See pages 15-16, 63-65, 75-77, and 85. It was published by the Princeton University Press, a very prestigious publishing house that certainly would not publish the theories of an antisemitic nut. The fact that Christians for centuries believed Jews killed Jesus becomes a lot more understandable when one sees that for centuries, every rabbi in Europe openly admitted that Jews killed Jesus, and furthermore declared that Jesus deserved it and the killers had nothing to be ashamed of. Let me repeat that, because so many people seem to have a hard time getting it through their heads: for centuries, every rabbi in Europe OPENLY ADMITTED that the Jewish authorities killed Jesus, and OPENLY DECLARED that killing Jesus was a good thing to do. This is why, for many centuries, European Christians had a policy of burning copies of the Babylonian Talmud whenever they found any. (Endnote 91.) But the Jews, undeterred, just kept making more copies.

What can one compare this to? The nearest modern equivalent would be if there was a well-organized minority group in the United States today, one or two percent of the population, that was constantly preaching that Martin Luther King was a disgusting pig who deserved to be killed, and that now he is burning in Hell. Obviously, if there was a minority group like that today, there would be tremendous hostility against it. Obviously, there would be job discrimination against such people, and there would be rumors that they were plotting terrorist attacks. So it should be no surprise that the anti-Jesus rhetoric of the Jews provoked hostility.

What if, hundreds of years ago, the rabbis of Europe had made it their practice, every Good Friday, to go to the local courthouse steps and publicly proclaim, "Jesus of Nazareth was innocent, and those who killed him committed a terrible sin!" I bet that would've gone a long way toward reducing anti-Semitism. But the rabbis did not do that, because that is not what they believed. They believed what the Babylonian Talmud said. As recently as the 1940s, when the famous Jewish writer Scholem Asch wrote a trilogy of novels that "depicted Jesus in a favorable light," many Jews were disgusted that he would do such a thing. (Endnote 92.)

Of course, it was not good for Christians to kill Jews just for being Jews. No pope, even in the middle ages, ever said it was. No pope ever said Jews should be given the choice of conversion or death. But when you look at the fact that the Judaists in those days believed that killing Jesus was a justifiable act, even a praiseworthy one, one cannot feel surprised that some Christians concluded that Judaists were rotten people. Perhaps this is one of the reasons why Shakespeare, when he wrote *The Merchant of Venice*, took it for granted that any Judaist must be a scoundrel.

Item 78: The Epistle to the Hebrews

On page 253 of *The God Delusion* (page 287 of the paperback) Dawkins says St. Paul wrote the Epistle to the Hebrews. The truth is that we don't know who wrote it. (Endnote 93.) St. Paul always started his epistles by stating his name, but the author of the Epistle to the Hebrews did not do that.

Item 79: Jews and Gentiles

On page 257 of *The God Delusion* (page 292 of the paperback) Dawkins says Jesus cared only about Jews, not about gentiles.

Once again, Dawkins is lying. Look at the Gospel of Mark, which, the experts say, was the first of the four gospels to be written. In chapter 13, verse 10, Jesus says that before the end of the world, "the good news must first be proclaimed to all the gentiles." Why preach to the gentiles if you don't care about them? In chapter 7, verses 24-30, a Canaanite woman, a gentile, is asking Jesus to expel a demon from her daughter. Jesus tests her faith, telling her it is not right to throw the food for the children to the dogs. She replies "Please Lord, even the dogs under the table eat the family's leavings." Jesus says, "For such a reply, be off now. The demon has already left your daughter." In chapter 7, verses 31-37, Jesus heals a deaf man in the "district of the Ten Cities" which was gentile territory, so the deaf man was almost certainly a gentile, and in chapter 5, verses 1-20, Jesus heals a man possessed by demons in that same district. Then in chapter 8, verses 1-9 Jesus multiplies loaves and fishes to feed four thousand people, also in the district of the Ten Cities. Why work miracles in gentile territory if you don't care about gentiles?

Next, look at the Gospel of Matthew. In chapter 12, verse 21, it says about Jesus, "In his name, the Gentiles will find hope." In chapter 12, verses 17 and 18, it says about Jesus, "This was to fulfill what had been said through Isaiah the prophet: 'Here is my servant whom I have chosen, my loved one in whom I delight. I will endow him with my spirit and he will proclaim justice to the Gentiles.'"

So why would anyone think Jesus didn't care about gentiles? Dawkins is talking nonsense.

Item 80: Ireland

On pages 260-262 of *The God Delusion* (pages 294-296 of the paperback) Dawkins talks about Protestants and Catholics fighting each other in Northern Ireland. No Catholic or Protestant bishop has endorsed the actions of any violent group in Ireland in the last sixty years, but Dawkins makes a subtler point: groups of people often fight over trivial differences, therefore all differences are bad, because they can lead to fighting, therefore society would be better if all religious people would become atheists.

If that is true, can't Dawkins see that by advocating atheism, he is just adding one more faction to the mix? I heard years ago that King Philip II of Spain also believed it was inevitable that people who belonged to different religions would constantly fight each other, but the conclusion that Philip II drew from this was that he should crush heresy and allow only one religion to exist in the lands that he ruled.

In modern times, didn't two atheists, Hitler and Stalin, fight the biggest war in human history against each other? Somehow atheism did not bring peace to eastern Europe. Dawkins, of course, refuses to face that fact.

But Claus von Stauffenberg, the man who tried to assassinate Hitler with a bomb in 1944, was a Catholic. The night before he blew up Hitler's bunker, he went to confession. (Endnote 94.) Dawkins, of course, doesn't talk about that. But if a secular humanist had tried to kill Hitler, Dawkins and his buddies would talk about that endlessly.

Now, it certainly is true that people will fight over trivial differences. Years ago in the United States, it was common for teenagers to form gangs, based on ethnicity, and fight each other, just like in the movie *West Side Story*. But it never occurs to Dawkins that if there were a significant number of atheists in Northern Ireland, they might fight too. The Catholics of Northern Ireland feel oppressed, discriminated against in employment and harassed by the police. That is why British left-wingers, such as Jeremy Corbyn, used to support the so-called Catholic side in that struggle. (Endnote 95.) Isn't it possible that atheists, if they felt oppressed, might resort to violence too? In Dawkins's opinion, apparently, the answer is no, that is simply not possible. Atheists, he apparently thinks, will never fight, no matter how oppressed they are. He never explains why he thinks that way, because he can't: there is no logical reason for thinking that way.

Item 81: Men, Women, and Darwin

On page 271 of *The God Delusion* (page 307 of the paperback) Dawkins says it is because of the theory of evolution, not the Bible, that we believe men and women share "common humanity." That is ridiculous. Is there no lie Dawkins won't tell? The Bible never says women aren't human. In chapter 3 of the Epistle to the Galatians, St. Paul stresses that "There does not exist among you Jew or Greek, slave or freeman, male or female. All are one in Christ Jesus." And in chapter 3 of the first letter of Peter, Peter writes, "You husbands, too, must show consideration for those who share your lives. Treat women with respect as the weaker sex, heirs just as much as you to the gracious gift of life."

Darwin, on the other hand, was certain that women were, on the average, intellectually inferior to men. Look at this statement that he made:

> "To avoid enemies, or to attack them with success, to capture wild animals, and to invent and fashion weapons, requires the aid of the higher mental faculties, namely, observation, reason, invention, or imagination. These various faculties will thus have been continually put to the test, and selected during manhood. . . . Thus man has ultimately become superior to woman." (Endnote 96.)

Isn't it amazing how rarely Darwin's fans mention that statement? Carl Sagan and Ann Druyan, in their book, *Shadows of Forgotten Ancestors*, talk on and on about what a wonderful guy they think Darwin was, but they never mention his sexism. They sweep that under the rug.

Item 82: A Progressive Trend?

On page 271 of *The God Delusion* (page 307 of the paperback) Dawkins says there is a "progressive trend" in the morality of the human race, which is his way of saying he thinks the moral behavior of the human race is better now than it was in the past, and despite occasional setbacks, has continued to improve.

I don't think that is true, but, to be fair to Dawkins, some of the evidence that I will discuss did not yet exist at the time when he made that statement.

First, consider this. Several years ago, the famous film director Roman Polanski raped a 13-year-old girl in California, but he jumped bond and escaped from the United States without spending a day in prison. In 2009, he was finally re-arrested, and for no good reason, many secularists in the cultural elite rallied to his defense. Woody Allen, Martin Scorsese, Debra Winger, Salman Rushdie, Milan Kundera, Pedro Almodovar, and Costa-Gavras all denounced the arrest. So did the French foreign minister and the French culture minister. They seemed to sincerely believe that just because Polanski has made some good films over the years, he deserves to get off scot-free after raping a child. (Endnote 97.)

When has anything like this been heard of before? When, in 1949, 1959, or 1969, did respectable members of society stand up and publicly declare that a man who raped a child should not be punished in any way? It is impossible to imagine anyone with any significant standing in society publicly saying that in those days. Then as now, many people did rotten things and covered them up, but they were never so brazen that they openly insisted that the rotten behavior deserved no punishment. One must conclude that some of these Hollywood glitterati types have become so degenerate that they honestly believe they should be allowed to do whatever they want.

Second, look at Gerhard Schroeder, a secular socialist politician and former chancellor of Germany. After leaving office, he took a high-paying job with Gazprom, a company controlled by the Russian government, headed at the time (and now) by Vladimir Putin. (Endnote 98.) What that means is that basically, Schroeder joined the Mafia. Putin is nothing but a gangster. He and his cronies steal everything they can get their hands on in Russia, and kill anyone who dares to complain.

In all the years since 1900, I can't think of any other time when a freely-elected leader of a major country was so degenerate, so completely uninterested in morality, that after he left office he openly accepted a lucrative job offer from a cold-blooded murderer such as Vladimir Putin. I know world leaders sometimes have to maintain friendly relations with unsavory characters. Such is international diplomacy. For example, for the sake of world peace, American presidents of both parties have turned a blind eye to China's brutal occupation of Tibet. But that is very different than being willing to work for a cold-blooded murderer, just to get a fat paycheck.

Third, James Stewart, one of America's most prominent investigative journalists, wrote a book about perjury a few years ago called *Tangled Webs*, in which he discussed some recent high-profile perjurers, such as Martha Stewart and Bernard Madoff. In the introduction to the book, on page xiv, he writes, "Mounting evidence suggests that the broad public commitment to telling the truth under oath has been breaking down, eroding over recent decades, a trend that has been accelerating in recent years." He admits that no statistics exist on this point, so one can't be certain it is true, but then says:

> "But prosecutors have told me repeatedly that a surge of concerted, deliberate lying by a different class of criminal – sophisticated, educated, affluent, and represented in many cases by the best lawyers – threatens to swamp the legal

system, and undermine the prosecution of white-collar crime. ... 'It's nearing a crisis,' James Comey, the former deputy attorney general and U.S. Attorney who prosecuted Martha Stewart, told me."

It is surely true that the influence of Christianity on American society has been waning in recent decades. I don't think it is surprising that Americans have become less honest at the same time.

Fourth, look at pages 53-56 of the book *How Israel Lost: The Four Questions*, by the prominent journalist Richard Ben Cramer. Cramer describes how Prime Minister Yitzhak Rabin was driven out of office in the 1970s because his wife was found to have a secret bank account in the United States containing twenty thousand dollars. People assumed that the money had to have been gotten in some kind of sleazy way. But a few decades later, Prime Minister Ariel Sharon was found to have received a secret, illegal $1.5 million loan from a foreign businessman, and he was not driven out of office. Instead, he was easily re-elected. Cramer asked a "distinguished" Israeli journalist named Sever Plotzker why Sharon was able to get away with doing something that was far more flagrant than the thing Rabin did. Plotzker said, "The standards have changed." Cramer also talked to a certain businesswoman about this scandal. She told him that the early Zionists were idealistic and cared first and foremost about what was good for the country, but now all that anyone seems to care about is money money money.

Fifth, Thomas L. Friedman, the famous foreign correspondent, has pointed out recently that democracy and human rights have not been faring well in the world in recent years. (Endnote 99.) "Democracy is in recession," he dolefully notes.

Sixth, there is absolutely no evidence that China is improving. The atheists who rule China didn't give a hoot about human rights back when Dawkins was writing *The God Delusion*, and they still don't. Yet, economically, China is growing stronger every day, and its population is so large that there is reason to believe that it will eventually become the most powerful country on Earth.

Seventh, *Psychology Today* magazine reported on page 69 of its December 2013 issue that in 1967, 86 percent of college freshmen said in a survey that "developing a meaningful philosophy of life" was an essential life goal. In 2004, only 42 percent of freshmen said that. The goal that became more popular was "being well-off financially."

So I'm afraid Dawkins is wrong. When you look at the morality of the human race, the trends are not good.

Item 83: Dawkins Ignores the Facts

On page 288 of *The God Delusion* (page 325-326 of the paperback) Dawkins rants about how awful he thinks the religious right is. Somehow he never finds time to complain about the bloody-handed atheists who brutally rule Russia, China and North Korea.

He quotes some of the more extreme things said by the religious right. One could just as easily indict atheism by quoting some of the more extreme things said by atheist radicals over the years. For example, Bernardine Dohrn, a member of a left-wing group called the Weather Underground, said about the murders committed by Charles Manson's gang, "Dig it, first they killed the pigs, then they ate dinner in the same room with them, then they even shoved a fork into a victim's stomach! Wild!" (Endnote 100. For those of you who don't remember the slang of the 1960s, "dig it" meant "that's good," or "I like it.") Jerry Rubin, a famous left-wing radical who co-founded a group called the Yippies, told an audience of 1,500 on a college campus in 1970, "The first part of the Yippie program is to kill your parents. And I mean that quite literally, because until you're prepared to kill your parents, you're not ready to change this country. Our parents are our first oppressors." (Endnote 101.) I've never heard anybody say Dohrn and Rubin were religious in any way.

Dohrn and Rubin were so disgusted by American society that they wanted a revolution, and they didn't see any reason why they should eschew violence. For some people, at least, that is the kind of thinking that atheism leads to.

And as I said earlier in this book, the atheist George Orwell was so remarkably callous that he actually wanted World War Two to be a long war, so the British people would suffer greatly and would therefore demand, as a reward for their sufferings, that Britain become a socialist society. (Endnote 102.)

All over the world, people were hoping and praying for a short war, so their loved ones would come home safely, but this atheist Orwell was hoping for a long war. But Dawkins never criticizes Orwell.

As I have also previously mentioned, if you want to talk about people desiring mass death, look at a biology professor named Eric Pianka. He has publicly declared that he would be glad if an epidemic wiped out 90 percent of the human race, as long as he and his buddies were among the survivors, because that would cut down on the amount of environmental damage done by the human race. (Endnote 103.) And I bet he is not the only environmentalist who thinks that way.

Dawkins does mention, on pages 325-331 of *The God Delusion* (pages 366-372 of the paperback) that a British atheist psychologist named Nicholas Humphrey thinks "we as a society have a duty" to prevent children from being taught beliefs that Humphrey thinks are silly, such as astrology or the literal truth of the Bible. In fact, on page 329 (page 370 of the paperback) Dawkins quotes Humphrey as saying that the Amish and the Hasidic Jews are among those whom he thinks should not be allowed to teach their beliefs to their children, which, one has to assume, means Humphrey wants to take children away from Amish and Hasidic Jewish parents. I think it is safe to say the average American would be disgusted to hear anyone advocate Humphrey's views, but Dawkins, apparently, is unperturbed. He will rant all day about how awful he thinks the religious right is, but he doesn't condemn Humphrey's views.

Item 84: Gays

On pages 289-291 of *The God Delusion* (page 326-329 of the paperback) Dawkins complains about discrimination against gays, and blames it on religion. I'm not so sure. The Bible condemns adultery just as strongly as it condemns homosexuality, if not more so, yet the animosity toward adulterers has never been nearly as strong as the animosity toward gays. Why is that? I don't know. Some of it surely is just the ordinary desire of immature people to be mean to anyone who is different. A junior high school bully is going to be mean to a homosexual, just as he is also going to be mean to someone who is overweight or has a bad case of acne. And maybe some of the hostility toward gays comes from men who, in boyhood, were raped. Would it surprise anyone to hear that boys who were raped sometimes grow up to be men who hate gays?

The simple fact is that one need not be religious to find gays disgusting. Fidel Castro and Mao Zedong, two of the most prominent atheists in the twentieth century, were also anti-gay. Castro had a policy of keeping the gays locked up. Mao ordered his followers to castrate convicted homosexuals in public ceremonies. (Endnote 104.)

And take a look at this passage from pages 88-89 of William Poundstone's biography of Carl Sagan, about Sagan and his eldest son Dorion: "In high school, Dorion became friends with a gay classmate. A worried Carl sat him down and lectured him that homosexuality was not the way the species propagated itself. He invoked natural selection, not Leviticus, as the basis for his disapproval."

Or look at this statement from the famous atheist philosopher Bertrand Russell. In a letter to a friend, Russell said about himself and the famous atheist novelist D.H. Lawrence, "Lawrence has the same feeling against sodomy as I have; you had nearly made me believe there is no great harm in it, but I have reverted; & all examples I know confirm me in thinking it sterilising." (Endnote 105.)

Or look at the fact that the famous atheist John Lennon, in an interview in 1970, made a caustic remark about Mick Jagger and his "fag dancing." (Endnote 106.) He also thought it was funny to deliberately annoy the Beatles' manager, Brian Epstein, who was gay, by singing the words "Baby, you're a rich fag Jew," instead of "Baby, you're a rich man too," when rehearsing the song "Baby You're a Rich Man." (Endnote 107.)

Or look at the fact that a survey taken a few years ago in China found that, though few Chinese are religious, there was much less tolerance for gays and lesbians in China than in the United States. (Endnote 108.)

Or look at the fact that the pagan Romans, long before Jesus was born, considered consensual homosexual activity disgusting in some circumstances (but not in others.) You can read about this in Craig Williams's book *Roman Homosexuality*. Pagan Roman attitudes about sex were very different than the way we think today. Pagan Roman men saw nothing wrong with a rich man raping his slaves, both male and female, both adult and minor, but they had nothing but contempt for a free man who let himself be anally penetrated. It was perfectly legal in ancient Rome for a woman to work as a prostitute, but homosexual prostitution was illegal. (Endnote 109.) In ancient Athens, homosexual prostitution was legal, but any man who did it was forbidden, for the rest of his life, to vote, or hold public office, or give a speech in the public assembly. (Endnote 110.)

Let me also point out a brouhaha that erupted a few years ago when someone made a cellphone video of Paris Hilton in the backseat of a cab, talking about how she thought gay men were "disgusting." Their promiscuity offended her. She called them "the horniest people in the world" and concluded "most of them probably have AIDS." (Endnote 111.) One must admit that promiscuity is common among gay men. Some women find that disgusting.

In the public high school I attended back in the 1970s, anti-gay thugs certainly existed. In fact, I strongly suspect that some of them would've gladly killed gays, if there had been no chance of being arrested for it. But the important fact is that the anti-gay thugs were not religious. They were the kind of people who never had the slightest desire to set foot inside a church. Just look at the two men who killed Matthew Shepard. Neither one of them was a churchgoer or a religious person. (Endnote 112.)

Let's also look at NAMBLA, the North American Man-Boy Love Association, an organization of gay men who want to legalize sexual intercourse between adult men and minors. I suspect there are a lot of atheists and agnostics in that organization. In fact, it wouldn't surprise me if every single member of NAMBLA was an atheist or agnostic. Is Dawkins going to talk about them? When he gets done quoting anti-gay statements from conservative preachers, does he quote NAMBLA leaders talking about how wonderful it would be to legalize sex between adults and minors? No, he doesn't do that. If he thinks anti-gay statements are appalling, doesn't he think NAMBLA statements are appalling too? Obviously, his policy is to not let his readers see appalling statements from atheist groups.

(Someone has told me that NAMBLA has disbanded, because the members became tired of the animosity they were attracting. But even if the organization no longer exists, I doubt that the ex-members have changed their minds.)

Item 85: Capital Punishment

On page 291 of *The God Delusion* (page 329 of the paperback) Dawkins complains that the religious right supports capital punishment.

As I said earlier in this chapter, a few years after Dawkins's book was published, Robert D. Putnam and David E. Campbell, two highly-regarded social science professors, published a book called *American Grace: How Religion Divides and Unites Us*. In it, on page 386, they say their survey found that the most religious quintile of Americans and the least religious quintile were equally likely to support capital punishment.

Of course, another thing to remember is that capital punishment is logical. What could be more logical than getting rid of troublemakers? Can't Dawkins see that? He says he wants people to be more logical, but when they are, he is horrified. In a room full of witnesses, Sirhan Sirhan killed Robert Kennedy. There is no doubt about his guilt. What logical reason is there to not execute Sirhan for this? What logical purpose is served by letting the guy stay alive, eating three meals per day at taxpayer expense? There may be emotional or religious reasons, but there are surely no logical ones.

One sees this a lot. Liberals say, "Be like Socrates! Question everything!" But when you question liberal dogmas, they're horrified.

Item 86: Alan Turing

On page 289 of *The God Delusion* (page 327 of the paperback) Dawkins blames Christianity for the fact that Alan Turing, a brilliant pioneer in the computer field, was arrested for homosexual activity, and was given a choice between prison or hormone treatments that would've abolished his sex drive. Dawkins says Turing responded to this situation by committing suicide by eating an apple that he had injected with cyanide.

Dawkins is not telling the whole story. One can read about this case in an article by Christian Caryl in the February 5, 2015 issue of the *New York Review of Books*. Caryl concludes that there are strong reasons for believing that Turing did not commit suicide. (The article about Turing in Wikipedia says the same thing.) Turing was found dead with a half-eaten apple beside him, and his death was indeed ruled a suicide, but he left no suicide note, and his mother says he did not seem despondent in the days before his death. In fact, he left on his desk a list of things he was planning to do next week. Dawkins claims Turing injected that apple with cyanide, but the truth is that the police never tested that apple to see if it was poisoned. As a hobby, Turing liked to gold-plate things, and one uses cyanide as part of that process, so he may have died from accidentally inhaling cyanide fumes. A philosophy professor who has looked into the case believes the autopsy evidence is more consistent with inhaling cyanide than with eating it.

The biggest problem with the theory that Turing committed suicide is the fact he died more than two years after he was convicted of homosexual activity, after the hormone treatments were completed. If a fellow is going to commit suicide over something like that, wouldn't you expect him to do it around the time he was arrested, or around the time he was convicted? Isn't that when a person would feel most upset about the incident?

And lastly, it is simply silly to blame Christianity for the fact that the British government forced hormone treatments on gays. As I said before, the Bible condemns adultery just as much as it condemns homosexual activity, yet adulterers were not forced to undergo hormone treatments. Obviously, it wasn't the Bible that was causing Britain's lawmakers to be horrified by homosexuality.

And let's also ask, if scientists are such wonderful people, why didn't the scientists of Great Britain rush to the defense of their buddy Turing? Why didn't they threaten to go on strike if the government didn't drop the charges? Apparently it never occurs to Dawkins that they could've done that. Were British scientists really such gutless wimps that they were willing to let their colleague be persecuted that way? Look at the fact that in 1967, a theology professor named Charles Curran at the Catholic University of America was denied tenure because of his views on birth control, and the entire faculty went on strike to demand that he be given tenure. After a week, the administration relented and gave Curran tenure. (Endnote 113.) Look at the Freedom Riders in the United States, a small group of people who were willing to put their lives on the line because they would not tolerate racial segregation for one more minute. (And many of them payed a high price too, suffering severe injuries at the hands of white supremacists. You can read about them by looking up "Freedom Riders" in Wikipedia.) Why didn't the scientists of Great Britain show a little courage? The answer is obvious: the scientists of Great Britain were logical, and it isn't logical to take risks to help others. But Dawkins can't bear to admit that.

Of course, another thing to remember is that the best psychiatrists in the English-speaking world in those days believed gays and lesbians were severely deranged people who were a menace to society. (Endnote 114.) Maybe the scientists of Great Britain assumed that the psychiatrists were right, and therefore thought it was right to force those hormone treatments on Turing. But Dawkins never considers that possibility.

Item 87: Again, Dawkins Feels No Need for Evidence

On page 88 of *The God Delusion* (page 112 of the paperback) Dawkins says George W. Bush said once that God told him to invade Iraq. Dawkins doesn't state his source of information for this claim. He wants his readers to just take it on faith.

Think about that. Dawkins makes a drastic accusation like this, and he doesn't even try to back it up with evidence. Does he really think that is the way a decent man acts?

If you check the Proquest Newspaper Database, you will find that a newspaper called the *Irish Examiner* reported on October 7, 2005, that a Palestinian politician named Nabil Shaath had recently claimed that Bush, in a private meeting with the Palestinian prime minister, said God told him to invade Iraq. Maybe that is what Dawkins is referring to. But the fact that the leading newspapers of the world did not pick up the story should've made Dawkins see that the best journalists did not consider the story credible. The Bush administration refused to comment on this news report, on the grounds that there is a long-standing American policy of never discussing private conversations between the president and other world leaders. The rationale for this policy is the fact that the president and other world leaders will not be able to discuss their problems frankly, and consider unconventional solutions, if they are worried that their statements will end up in the newspapers.

So, apparently, Dawkins thinks there is no chance that Nabil Shaath simply misunderstood something Bush said, and no chance that Nabil Shaath simply lied. I beg to differ. Palestinian politicians do not have a good track record for honesty. In an astonishingly brazen lie, they insist that there never was a Jewish temple on the Temple Mount in Jerusalem. The director of one of the mosques that stands on the

Temple Mount today told the Israeli journalist Gershom Gorenberg, "This is an Islamic holy site. It never has been related to anything else." (Endnote 115.) Many Muslims in the Middle East insist the Holocaust never happened. They claim Israeli agents go to Arab countries and hand out free candy to children that causes sterility. In 1973, when the Yom Kippur War broke out, the Arabs insisted that Israel started it, something which no American or European historian believes today. So why in the world should we believe Nabil Shaath? It is astonishing that Dawkins thinks Shaath is a credible source of information. It is no better than if Dawkins was to say he believes something because he heard it once from a wino in a tavern.

Item 88: Dawkins Denounces Mother Teresa

On page 292 of *The God Delusion* (page 330 of the paperback) Dawkins announces that it was ridiculous for Mother Teresa to say "The greatest destroyer of peace is abortion." He says that because she thought that way, she should not have been given the Nobel Peace Prize.

I think it is safe to say that the average American would say Dawkins is being pretty narrow-minded here. Even most people who want to keep abortion legal find it easy to see why some people think it is murder. Hillary Clinton certainly wants to keep abortion legal, but she would never in a million years say Mother Teresa did not deserve the Nobel Peace Prize.

Dawkins goes on to call Mother Teresa "sanctimoniously hypocritical." He presents no evidence to support that accusation. He claims the evidence is in an obscure book, written by Christopher Hitchens, that few public libraries in the United States bothered to buy. I've never even seen a copy of that book, but the *Guardian*, the most prominent socialist newspaper in Great Britain, the kind of newspaper that a socialist like Dawkins would surely trust, published a review of it in their November 3, 1995 issue. The reviewer, a lady named Catherine Bennett, concluded that the book is much ado about nothing, that Hitchens has no evidence that Mother Teresa ever did anything seriously bad. If Dawkins thinks otherwise, why can't he give us a quick paragraph to tell us what some of the evidence is? Doesn't Dawkins know that no decent man makes an accusation like that without backing it up with evidence? Of course he knows that, but he has no desire to be a decent man.

I know one of Hitchens's complaints was that sometimes Mother Teresa accepted donations from crooks. If that is true, she wasn't alone.

A few years ago, Oxford University accepted a $100 million donation from a crooked Russian billionaire named Leonard Blavatnik, while Harvard accepted a $50 million donation from him, and Yale accepted $10 million. (Endnote 116.) So, if Dawkins condemns Mother Teresa for accepting contributions from crooks, I wonder if he will condemn Oxford, Harvard and Yale too. Yale University has also accepted big donations from the Sackler family, even though the Sacklers made their money by creating the opioid crisis that has killed thousands of Americans in recent years. (Endnote 117.) Is Dawkins going to condemn Yale for that too? If John Doe owns a grocery store where he sells, among other things, cigarettes and beer, does that mean all charities should refuse to accept donations from John Doe?

Item 89: Anti-Abortion Terrorism

On page 292 of *The God Delusion* (page 330 of the paperback) Dawkins claims anti-abortion activist Randall Terry once said "Yes, hate is good," and some other bizarre things. Dawkins's source of information for this claim is the website of some atheist group. I recently looked at that website. I get the impression that the group is defunct, because the website hasn't been updated since 2010. But in any case, why should we believe that website? Doesn't Dawkins know that lies are common on the Internet?

The important fact here is that the number of people killed by the anti-abortion movement in the United States in the last fifty years is quite small. According to the article "Anti-Abortion Violence" in Wikipedia, there have been only eleven. (And Dawkins never claims that the number is greater than eleven.) Compare that to the 168 killed by the agnostic Timothy McVeigh, and look at all the people killed for no good reason in recent years by the atheists who rule Russia, China, and North Korea. But that is a fact that Dawkins doesn't want his readers to think about. I'm sure more than eleven people have been killed in the United States in the last fifty years in swimming pool accidents, but I don't hear Dawkins saying we should ban swimming pools. Compare it to the thirty-nine people who were killed in a soccer riot in Belgium in 1985. (Endnote 118.) I don't hear the militant atheists saying we should outlaw soccer.

We certainly know that some spectacular murders were committed by atheists and agnostics such as Lee Harvey Oswald, James Earl Ray, Giuseppe Zangara and Timothy McVeigh. We don't know how many murders are committed by atheists in the United States each year, because journalists rarely bother to tell us whether this or that person who has been convicted of murder is an atheist.

Item 90: Revolutionaries

On pages 295-296 of *The God Delusion* (pages 334-335 of the paperback) Dawkins condemns the killing of abortion doctors and says one should not take the law into one's own hands.

Well, I certainly don't approve of killing abortion doctors, but I wonder if this means Dawkins also thinks it was bad for John Brown to try to start a slave revolt. I also wonder about the fact that Dawkins admires Thomas Jefferson, despite the fact that Jefferson was perfectly willing to kill people during the Revolutionary War, just because he had a disagreement with the British king over taxes. Is Dawkins going to condemn Jefferson for that? The question never seems to enter his head.

Item 91: The Philosophy of Abortion

On pages 298-300 of *The God Delusion* (pages 337-339 of the paperback) Dawkins shows us how good he is at missing the point. Apparently some anti-abortion activists have said that if you think it is good to perform an abortion on a woman who has tuberculosis and whose children all have serious health problems, that means you would've aborted Beethoven. Dawkins first says that story gets the facts wrong about Beethoven's siblings, and then goes on to approvingly quote a person named Peter Medawar as saying the anecdote proves nothing anyway, because "the world is no more likely to be deprived of a Beethoven by abortion than by chaste abstinence from intercourse."

I have no idea what the truth is about the health of Beethoven's mother and siblings, but it should be obvious to anyone that the point that the anti-abortion people are making in this anecdote is not that the world needs more people because some of them will be extremely talented. The point is that once a child is conceived, even if the child is handicapped, that doesn't necessarily mean we will all be better off if the child is aborted. The point is that we shouldn't call people worthless when they haven't even been born yet. It is amazing that Medawar and Dawkins can't see something that is so obvious. Would Medawar and Dawkins look a guy with cerebral palsy in the eye and tell him that his life is worthless and that they wish he had never been born?

Well, maybe Dawkins would. A few years ago, he declared publicly that if a lady is pregnant and knows the baby has Down's syndrome, then she should have an abortion, that it is "immoral" for her to give birth to such a baby. (Endnote 119.) Apparently Dawkins would look a person with Down's syndrome in the eye and say, "Bringing you into the world was an immoral act."

Item 92: The Rights of Chimps

On page 300-301 of *The God Delusion* (page 339-340 of the paperback) Dawkins says that because of evolution, we are related to chimps and gorillas and all other animals, and therefore we shouldn't give "uniquely special rights" to humans. He never explains what "uniquely special rights" he is talking about. He prefers to keep it vague. Does he want to give gorillas the right to vote? Or does he merely want to make it illegal to kill gorillas? It already is, at least in the United States, except to defend a human. Is he saying we should make it illegal to use chimps and gorillas in medical experiments, even when there is no good way to do the research without them? Doesn't that seem like an anti-science attitude? If that is what he means, isn't he afraid people will accuse him of blocking scientific progress? But he keeps his statement so vague that it is impossible to know what he means. What is the use of talking if you aren't going to make yourself clear?

Let me point out here that there is an atheist philosophy professor named Alex Rosenberg who wrote a book years ago called *The Atheist's Guide to Reality*, in which he said that one cannot logically prove that one's ideas about morality are better than anyone else's ideas about morality, therefore the word "morality" doesn't mean anything. Rosenberg bluntly declared that there is no logical reason to not grab people at random off the street and kill them. (I have a chapter about Rosenberg's book in my book, *Darwin Wanted to Exterminate the Blacks, and Other Facts About Famous Atheists.*)

Let me also point out that the famous atheist scientist Edward O. Wilson said years ago that morality is just whatever most people say it is. (Endnote 120.) Therefore one has to assume that if most people on Earth wanted to exterminate the gays, or enslave the blacks, or use animals in extremely painful scientific experiments, then Wilson would say that is what morality is.

So what logical reason can Dawkins give for saying we should care about the rights of gorillas and chimps? None. He can't prove that they deserve rights any more than I can prove Jesus walked on water. He is simply taking it on faith. Why doesn't he admit that?

Dawkins says he wants people to be logical. Can't he see that it is logical to use animals in any way that benefits us? I oppose cruelty to animals, but my reasons are purely emotional and I'm not going to pretend otherwise. Dawkins's reasons are also purely emotional, but he can't bear to admit that. If he did, people would say to him, "If it is okay for you to use emotional thinking to believe in animal rights, then it is okay for me to use emotional thinking to believe in Christianity." Dawkins would have no answer to that.

Item 93: Zionism

On page 302 of *The God Delusion* (page 341 of the paperback) Dawkins says there are Christians in the United States who think "Israel has the God-given right to all the lands of Palestine." I guess there are some American Christians who think that way. But then Dawkins says those people have a "powerful influence" on American foreign policy in the Middle East. Wrong again, Mr. Dawkins. George W. Bush himself publicly endorsed the idea that there should be an independent Palestinian state on the West Bank and Gaza Strip. (Endnote 121.)

Obviously this "powerful influence" that Dawkins was talking about was actually no influence at all. Take note of the fact that Bush announced his support for a Palestinian state in 2002, and Dawkins did not publish *The God Delusion* until 2006. Why did he not know that Bush had endorsed creation of a Palestinian state? Most likely he knew it perfectly well, but was simply hoping he could fool his readers.

Item 94: Muslims and Terrorism

On page 303 of *The God Delusion* (page 343 of the paperback) Dawkins talks about the Muslims who carried out the suicide bombings in the London subway in 2005 that killed fifty-two people. He says "Only religious faith is a strong enough force to motivate such utter madness in otherwise sane and decent people."

Why does he talk about "religious faith," as if all religions are the same? When have any Christians ever volunteered to be suicide bombers? Never that I've heard. Dawkins mentions no such case. But the atheist Leon Czolgosz killed President McKinley, even though he knew he would surely be caught in the act and executed. And the atheist Giuseppe Zangara fired five shots at Franklin Roosevelt one day in 1932, and missed every time, but killed the mayor of Chicago who was standing next to FDR. Zangara was arrested and executed, as he surely knew he would be. And the atheist Lee Harvey Oswald killed President Kennedy, even though he surely knew his chances of avoiding arrest were extremely small. Why did they do it? Because they had strongly-held political beliefs. Czolgosz and Zangara were anarchists who hated the rich, and hated the politicians who, in their opinion, served the rich. Oswald was a communist who admired Fidel Castro and believed Castro's claim that Kennedy was trying to kill him, therefore Oswald killed Kennedy to save the life of his hero. Why does Dawkins find it so hard to imagine that political beliefs can motivate an atheist to volunteer for a suicide mission?

Item 95: Dawkins Lies About Thomas Paine

On page 38 of *The God Delusion* (page 59 of the paperback) Dawkins claims that Thomas Paine "died in penury, abandoned (with the honorable exception of Jefferson) by political former friends embarrassed by his anti-Christian views." (In the paperback, he leaves out the words "in penury.")

That is dead wrong. Why can't Dawkins get the facts straight? It is true that Paine didn't have much money at the time of his death, but whose fault was that? Read the book *Tom Paine: A Political Life*, by history professor John Keane, and you will see that from 1794, when he was released from prison in France, until his death in 1809, Paine barely did a lick of work. He devoted his time to writing newspaper screeds about political and religious subjects, which earned him very little money, and when he ran low on funds he expected his friends to support him. Some of them did, for a while, but he was quarrelsome and a heavy drinker and just about everybody got tired of him eventually. In those days, the normal way to provide for your old age was to have children, but Paine never got around to doing that. (There were rumors that he had illegitimate children, but if he did, they never lifted a finger to help him.)

Look at page 430 of Keane's book and you will see that in 1796, Paine published a bitter personal attack on his ex-friend George Washington, which resulted in bitter counterattacks from Washington's supporters. Keane estimates on page 432 that this controversy may have hurt Paine's reputation in the United States more than his anti-Christian writings did. But Dawkins doesn't mention that.

And where does Dawkins get this stuff about Jefferson being Paine's only friend in his last years? When Paine returned to the United

States in 1802, Jefferson gave him a friendly welcome, but so did many other people. Paine wore out his welcome soon enough. One can read about it on pages 513-514 of Keane's book. In 1805 Paine sent Jefferson a letter, begging for money. Jefferson didn't even bother to reply. So Paine wrote again. Again, no reply from the sage of Monticello. In 1806, Paine sent another letter, this time asking for a government job. Jefferson replied that Paine's services were not needed. Then on page 530, Keane says in 1808 Paine sent a petition to Congress, asking for a government pension. He also wrote to Jefferson, asking Jefferson to try to get Congress to approve the pension request. Jefferson wrote back, saying he wasn't going to get involved and Congress was extremely unlikely to grant the request. Basically, Jefferson was telling Paine to take a hike. That was the last time Jefferson communicated with Paine in any way. So why on Earth does Dawkins think Jefferson never "abandoned" Paine? Is that just another lie that he found on some atheist website?

Item 96: The Atomic Bomb

On page 309 of *The God Delusion* (page 349 of the paperback) Dawkins approvingly quotes Victor Hugo as saying "In every village there is a torch – the teacher – and an extinguisher – the clergyman."

Dawkins has an attitude more common in the nineteenth century than the twenty-first: he assumes knowledge is always good. Hasn't he noticed that science gave us the atomic bomb? Doesn't he think we would be better off without it? Is he not concerned that our knowledge of genetic engineering will become so great that someday even people without much education, with fairly cheap equipment, will be able to cook up enough germs to kill millions of people? If he isn't worried about that, he should read the essay by the prominent physicist Martin Rees in the book *What Should We Be Worried About?* edited by John Brockman. Rees definitely is worried about that.

Knowledge without morality is dangerous. Dawkins ought to admit that.

Item 97: Dawkins Takes It on Faith

On page 306 of *The God Delusion* (page 346 of the paperback) Dawkins says we should never have faith in anything. Doesn't he see that he is contradicting himself? He wants us to take it on faith that chimps and gorillas deserve rights. He wants us to take it on faith that killing chimps and gorillas in medical experiments is evil. He wants us to take it on faith that all the statements he quotes from famous people are genuine. But then out of the other side of his mouth, Dawkins says we should take nothing on faith. How amusing. What he really means is that we shouldn't take anything on faith except the things he wants us to take on faith.

Item 98: Teaching Children

On page 308 of *The God Delusion* (page 347-348 of the paperback) Dawkins says it is bad for clergymen to teach children that faith is a virtue, because it "primes them" to commit terrorist acts for religious reasons.

I guess there must be quite a long list of things that Dawkins doesn't want taught to children. Don't teach them that Jesus was the son of God, because they might commit terrorist acts against people who don't believe that. Don't teach them that murder is bad, because they might try to kill abortion doctors. Don't teach them that businessman are destroying the environment, because they might commit terrorist acts against businessmen. Don't teach them that rape is bad, because they might want to kill rapists. Don't teach them that all humans are sisters and brothers, because then they might commit terrorist acts against politicians whom they consider intolerant. (That happened a few years ago in the Netherlands. A gay man named Pim Fortuyn got tired of being insulted by Muslim fundamentalists, so he went into politics and argued in favor of restricting Muslim immigration. Polls indicated that his message was quite popular and he was likely to do well in the upcoming elections. A white liberal, horrified that anyone would advocate restricting immigration, and horrified by any kind of discrimination, assassinated Fortuyn. You can read about this in the May 7, 2002 and April 16, 2003 issues of the *New York Times*.) Don't tell them to help the needy, because they might get angry at rich people who don't help the needy. (This too actually happened. John Lennon was murdered by a leftist who was angry at him because he had abandoned the hippie idealism of the 1960s and was living in luxury. See page 804 of *John Lennon: The Life*, by Philip Norman. And of course, there was certainly no shortage of left-wing terrorists in the twentieth century who wanted to kill the rich.)

Let's look at the guys in the Mafia. They certainly have faith in nothing. All they know is that they like to make money. So they are forming companies in Europe that bid on contracts to handle toxic waste. Then, to save money and boost their profit margins, they don't do the expensive work of disposing of the toxic waste safely. They just dump it in the Mediterranean Sea, or in poor African countries where environmental regulation is weak. This, of course, poisons the environment and leads to deaths and illnesses, but the Mafia men don't care about that. (Endnote 122.)

The Mafia men have faith in nothing. I guess those are the guys Dawkins likes best.

Look at Steve Jobs. He ignored faith and made the strictly logical decision that he could make billions of dollars by giving his workers in China pitifully low wages and lousy working conditions. (Endnote 123.) He saw no logical reason why he should care about his workers. Why can't Dawkins see that cruelty is often logical?

And what about Kathy Boudin? You can read about her in Wikipedia, and in the May 4, 1984 issue of the *New York Times*. She belonged to a terrorist group, and took part in a robbery that killed three people. She said she did it because of "my commitment to the black liberation struggle." Does that mean Dawkins thinks we shouldn't teach children to oppose racial discrimination, because then they might commit terrorist acts, as Kathy Boudin did?

And of course, let us remember that Dawkins himself admitted on page 215 (page 246 of the paperback) that hearing about the theory of evolution can cause people to believe in social Darwinism, which Dawkins and I both consider a bad thing. Of course, he had to admit that. It is common knowledge that Darwinism led to social Darwinism. Vernon Kellogg, a prominent American scientist who believed in evolution, was astonished to discover, when he visited Germany during World War One, that many German scientists thought it was obvious that the theory of evolution meant that Germany was morally justified in invading and conquering the weaker countries of Europe. (Endnote 124.) Therefore, if Dawkins is going to condemn the teaching of Christianity to children, on the grounds that it might lead to terrorism some day, that means that he must also condemn the teaching of evolution to children, on the grounds that it might lead to social Darwinism and the glorification of military conquest.

But Dawkins never thinks of that. It never enters his head.

Item 99: Atheist Terrorism

On page 304 of *The God Delusion* (page 344 of the paperback), Dawkins emphasizes that Christians who kill abortion doctors believe they are doing something good. This, Dawkins says, proves how evil Christianity is.

Well, let me point out again, Christianity motivated John Brown to break the law by trying to start a slave revolt in Virginia. Does Dawkins think that, too, means Christianity is evil?

Shortly after *The God Delusion* was published, a man in Colorado named Matthew Murray posted an anti-Christian rant on a website, then shot four people to death, two at a church, and two at a training center for Christian teachers. (Endnote 125.) Obviously Murray thought he was doing something good. Why else would he have done it? So does Dawkins think this proves atheism is evil?

In North Carolina in 2015, a militant atheist named Craig Stephen Hicks shot three Muslims to death for no good reason. (Endnote 126.) Does Dawkins think that proves atheism is evil?

As I said above, the leftist Kathy Boudin and her left-wing friends murdered three people in 1981, during a robbery. They thought they were fighting for human rights. In Italy in the 1970s and 1980s, a left-wing atheist terrorist group called the Red Brigades killed seventy-five people, including Aldo Moro, a former prime minister of Italy. The Red Brigades thought they were doing something good. In West Germany in the 1970s, a left-wing atheist terrorist group called the Baader-Meinhof gang killed thirty-four people. They too thought they were doing something good. Timothy McVeigh was an agnostic. (Endnote 127.) He thought he was a virtuous man who was fighting against an oppressive government. All the people I just listed thought they were standing up for justice and human rights. Does that mean Dawkins thinks we shouldn't teach children to care about justice and human rights? Logically, one would have to say yes, if you accept

Dawkins's basic belief that any idea that might lead to violence must not be taught to children.

And, as I said earlier, I could also talk about a bunch of guys named Jefferson, Washington, Adams and Hamilton who formed an army that killed thousands of people for secular political reasons during the American Revolution. They certainly killed far more people than the anti-abortion movement has in the United States. Is Dawkins going to condemn them too? Apparently the question never enters his head.

Perhaps Dawkins would argue that believing in justice and human rights is different than religion. Perhaps he would argue that justice and human rights can logically be proven to be good. If that is what he thinks, why doesn't he try to prove it? As I have already mentioned, the famous scientist Edward O. Wilson, whom Dawkins called "great," has said that morality is an "illusion." Wilson argued in the "Ethics and Religion" chapter of his book *Consilience* that a logical atheist must believe there are no eternal moral truths, that "morality" and "justice" and "human rights" are meaningless concepts, that something is bad only if most people think it is bad. This obviously means that Wilson thinks that if most people on Earth wanted to exterminate the gays or the Jews or any other group, there would be nothing wrong with that. And of course, as I said earlier, the atheist philosophy professor Alex Rosenberg, in his book *The Atheist's Guide to Reality*, reached the same conclusion: that morality is a meaningless word, that all ideas about morality are ridiculous.

Dawkins should admit the obvious: people who believe in justice and human rights are taking them on faith, just as much as Christians take the resurrection of Jesus on faith.

Item 100: Dawkins Ignores Logic

In Chapter 8 of *The God Delusion*, in the section called "Faith and the sanctity of human life," Dawkins admits that some people argue that if we keep abortion legal, we will eventually legalize infanticide too. He makes no effort to answer that argument. He just changes the subject. So much for logic.

Or maybe Dawkins just isn't bothered by the thought of legalizing infanticide. After all, he will never again be an infant, so why should he care?

Item 101: Dawkins Denounces Islam

On pages 301-308 of *The God Delusion* (pages 341-348 of the paperback) Dawkins talks on and on about how evil he thinks Islam is, and he means all Islam, not just radical or fundamentalist Islam. Well then, does that mean he wants to ban Muslim immigration to his country? Quite a few people in Britain would like to do that. If you really think Islam is evil, then banning Muslim immigration is the logical thing to do, isn't it? But Dawkins says not a word about this. Why? Because he is a coward. What else can explain his refusal to confront the obvious question? He won't say that he wants to ban Muslim immigration to Britain, because then the Muslims (and maybe his liberal buddies too) would get angry at him, and he is too cowardly to face that. But he also won't say that he supports letting Muslims immigrate to Britain, because then people will ask him how in the world he can say that when he thinks Islam is evil, and he wouldn't be able to answer that question. So he just stands there like a scarecrow and says nothing.

Item 102: Dawkins Denounces Islam Again

On page 308 of *The God Delusion* (page 348 of the paperback), Dawkins complains that "faith" leads to suicide bombings. Oh really? When has Christianity led to suicide bombings? Never. He should be saying Islam leads to suicide bombings, not faith, but he can't bear to tell the truth.

Years after *The God Delusion* was published, Dawkins finally admitted that Islam causes more trouble in the world than Christianity does. In fact, he called Islam, "the greatest force for evil in the world today." (Endnote 128.) But he was wrong about that. Look at the way the atheists rule Russia, China, North Korea and other countries, and you will see that atheism is the greatest force for evil in the world today, or else greed is.

Item 103: Moral Principles

On pages 262-272 of *The God Delusion* (pages 298-308 of the paperback) Dawkins tells us what his moral principles are, but he never explains what intellectual process led him to adopt those principles. One has to suspect that that is because there was no process, that he simply adopted the views that were common in his social milieu, but that he doesn't want to admit that, because he is afraid that would make him look rather stupid. If you think logic is so wonderful, Mr. Dawkins, then give us logical reasons for your moral beliefs. Steve Jobs, a very smart guy, treated his workers in China like slaves so he could make billions of dollars. How would you logically prove to him that that was bad?

It is also interesting to see that Dawkins isn't willing to face up to the question of adultery. He says "Enjoy your own sex life (so long as it damages nobody else)," but he doesn't define "damage." Do you think adultery is bad or not, Mr. Dawkins? He is too cowardly to say. Einstein committed adultery many times, and that hurt his wife's feelings quite a lot, but Einstein saw no logical reason why he should care much about his wife's feelings. One wonders if Dawkins thinks the same way. Maybe that is why he has been divorced twice.

And finally, Mr. Dawkins, is it immoral for someone to spend a ton of money to buy a Porsche or a Rolls Royce in a world where so many people are needy? Dawkins never addresses that question. Has it never occurred to him? When I was in college, the campus socialists were constantly saying it is immoral that some people are rich. Living in Britain most of his life, Dawkins surely must have heard leftists saying things like that. Why doesn't he tell us whether he agrees with that idea? If you are going to talk seriously about morality in the modern world, it is an idea that you simply cannot ignore. You must either agree with it, or explain why you don't.

Item 104: The Definition of Indoctrination

On page 264 of *The God Delusion* (page 300 of the paperback) Dawkins says we should never "indoctrinate" children, we should instead let them "think for themselves." He doesn't explain what he means by that. He doesn't define "indoctrinate." If your 15-year-old says, "Ayn Rand is right. It is obvious that the most important thing in life is making money and having fun. I'm never going to donate one red cent to charity," does Dawkins sincerely believe that it would be bad to try to talk the kid out of that? If your 15-year-old says "I've decided Edward O. Wilson and Alex Rosenberg are right. Morality is just a stupid illusion. I'm never going to spend time thinking about it," does Dawkins think nothing should be done about that either? And if your 15-year-old says "Marx and Lenin were right. Capitalism is the root of all evil. We should kill all the businessmen," would Dawkins say there is no need to have a little talk with him about that?

What does Dawkins think a fellow should do if his 10-year-old son picks a fight with a boy at school and gives him a black eye? Just tell the kid, "Personally, I think that was not a good thing to do, but hey, I may be wrong, so you've got to decide this for yourself"? Is that really what Dawkins would say?

I suspect that what is going on here is that Dawkins thinks that when he and people like him talk to their children about their moral beliefs, that's just a reasonable discussion, but when people with whom he disagrees talk to their children about their moral beliefs, that's "indoctrination."

On the same page, Dawkins says we must teach children "how to evaluate evidence." Is that supposed to be a joke? Dawkins proves throughout the book that his method of evaluating evidence is to simply believe whatever pleases him and ignore the evidence that doesn't fit his preconceptions.

Item 105: The Sabbath

In *The God Delusion*, in the first section of Chapter 9, Dawkins complains about the fact that in Rome in the 1800s, a Jewish boy named Edgardo Mortara was taken away from his parents by the Catholic church and raised by nuns, because his parents' Catholic maid had baptized him one day, which made him a Christian. The pope at that time would not tolerate a Christian being raised by Jewish parents.

Dawkins thinks it was bad that the pope did that. Indeed it was. But then Dawkins goes the next mile and blames Judaism, because the only reason Edgardo's parents had a Catholic maid is because "The Jews needed servants whose religion didn't forbid them to work on the sabbath." Once again, Dawkins is wrong. The Jews didn't "need" such servants. After all, poor Jews got by with no servants at all. The wealthier Jews just wanted servants who would work on the Jewish sabbath, so, in hiring servants, they discriminated against their own people.

And it may be worth mentioning that Edgardo Mortara stayed in the Catholic fold in adulthood. He became a priest, and remained one until he died of old age. Dawkins doesn't mention that, but you can read about it in the book *The Kidnapping of Edgardo Mortara* by David Kertzer.

Item 106: Alfred Hitchcock

On page 318 of *The God Delusion* (page 357 of the paperback) Dawkins claims that Alfred Hitchcock, the famous filmmaker, believed it was terrible that so many children are taught the Catholic faith while growing up. Dawkins presents no evidence that Hitchcock thought this way. Once again, he expects his readers to just take it on faith. Furthermore, I don't see why Dawkins would think Hitchcock's opinion of the Catholic Church was worth hearing. Hitchcock was a great filmmaker, but he was a rotten human being. He told Tippi Hedron, an actress, that he would ruin her career if she didn't go to bed with him. (Endnote 129.)

Item 107: Intolerance

On pages 325-331 of *The God Delusion* (pages 366-372 of the paperback) Dawkins talks about the ideas of a British psychologist named Nicholas Humphrey, who thinks "we as a society have a duty" to prevent children from being taught beliefs that Humphrey thinks are silly, such as astrology or the literal truth of the Bible. In fact, on page 329 (page 370 of the paperback) Dawkins quotes Humphrey as saying that the Amish and the Hasidic Jews are among those whom he thinks should not be allowed to teach their beliefs to their children.

Can you imagine that scene? Can you imagine the police showing up in a Hasidic home or an Amish home to take the children away to some government group home, just because the government is dominated by people like Humphrey who don't like Hasidic Judaism or the Amish faith? Can you imagine the screaming and weeping that would ensue? For the foreseeable future, it is safe to say that Americans would find such scenes intolerable.

Isn't it astounding that this atheist Humphrey has declared war on the Amish, who have got to be the most harmless people in the entire United States?

Amazingly, Dawkins is such a coward that he never says whether or not he agrees with Humphrey. All he says, in conclusion, is that the idea of letting people raise their children in religions that he finds silly makes him "feel very queasy indeed."

And of course, Dawkins never thinks of the obvious fact that if the Constitution allows the government to take children away from the Amish and the Hasidim, then the Constitution will also allow the government to take children away from atheists. What's sauce for the goose is sauce for the gander, buddy. If you give the government tremendous power, don't be surprised if that power ends up being used against you someday.

Item 108: Physician-Assisted Suicide

On page 357 of *The God Delusion* (page 400 of the paperback) Dawkins says it is "enlightened" to allow physician-assisted suicide. He never discusses the most obvious secular objection: that nasty people will nag grandma into signing the suicide consent form just so they can inherit her money, or just because they are tired of spending every Sunday visiting her in the nursing home.

Dawkins blames religion for the fact that physician-assisted suicide is illegal in most places. He's right about that, in the sense that Christianity teaches that suicide is a sin, whereas the pagan Romans and Greeks didn't think there was anything so bad about it, but Dawkins fails to see that it is legal in few places because most people don't need it, so it never becomes an issue. If there were people in the United States who were screaming in pain day after day, begging to be allowed to die, journalists would start talking about that fact, and you can bet your life that physician-assisted suicide would be legalized, and some of the churches would drop their objections to it too.

But here's another thing Dawkins ought to consider. On page 229 of his book *The End of Faith*, Sam Harris mentions the fact that several years ago, when the Indian government changed the date for a civil service exam, a "wave" of people committed suicide in protest. (And what is even more astounding is that setting one's self on fire was the preferred method for protest suicide.) Harris was amazed that people would commit suicide over such a trivial matter.

This shows that when people start to think suicide is not immoral, some of them will commit suicide for the stupidest of reasons. Do we really want to let society go down that path?

Item 109: Dawkins Lies About Limbo

On page 401 of the paperback edition of *The God Delusion*, but nowhere in the hardcover edition, Dawkins declares that Pope Benedict XVI recently "abolished limbo." He wonders how Benedict could possibly think previous popes were wrong about limbo, when popes are supposed to be infallible.

Once again we see Dawkins shooting off his mouth without bothering to gather the facts first. Here's the background information. Theologians have long wondered what happened to babies who died before they could be baptized. Some speculated that there is a place called Limbo, that is a nice place, but not as good as Heaven, and that babies went to Limbo if they died before they could be baptized. The leaders of the Catholic Church never said that it was an official element of church doctrine. It was just an idea that some theologians had. In 2007, Pope Benedict XVI issued a statement that repeated that Limbo is not an official element of church doctrine, and never was, and that it is entirely possible that babies who die before they can be baptized go to Heaven. (Endnote 130.)

So Dawkins is wrong to say Benedict "abolished limbo." It was never an official part of church doctrine in the first place. No church council ever declared that it existed, and no pope ever said the Catholic people had to believe in it. The articles in the *New York Times* and the *Los Angeles Times* that I mentioned in the previous paragraph made that clear. Why does Dawkins talk about theology if he isn't going to take the time to understand it? Is reading a newspaper article and understanding it really too doggone difficult for Dawkins?

Item 110: Dawkins Lies About Purgatory

On page 360 of *The God Delusion* (page 403 of the paperback) Dawkins ridicules the idea of Purgatory and says the only reason Catholic theologians give for believing in it is because they pray for the dead, and there would be no point in praying for the dead if everyone goes to Heaven or Hell immediately after death.

Dawkins is either lying or has misunderstood something he read. The Catholic Church believes in Purgatory because it is implied in the Bible. The story is in the Old Testament, in verses 39 through 46 of chapter 12 of the Second Book of Maccabees. Some Jewish soldiers die in a battle, and the people assigned to gather their bodies and bury them find they are wearing "amulets sacred to the idols of Jamnia" under their tunics. It was sinful to wear such an amulet, so the Jewish commander, Judas Maccabeus, orders his troops to pray to God to forgive the sin of the dead men, and offers a sacrifice in Jerusalem to atone for the sin. Catholic theologians have reasoned that Judas Maccabeus was a great and holy man who surely wouldn't be mistaken about something like this, so they concluded that praying for the dead must be a virtuous thing to do. Praying for them would be futile if they were in Hell, and unnecessary if they were in Heaven, so they must be somewhere in between, which they labeled Purgatory.

Martin Luther and other Protestant leaders rejected this line of reasoning, because they didn't consider the Second Book of Maccabees to be part of the Bible. One of the little known facts about Christianity is that the Catholic Bible has several books that the Protestant Bible doesn't have.

Item 111: Dawkins Lies About Death

On page 361 of *The God Delusion* (page 405 of the paperback) Dawkins claims that the belief that death ends life completely is good, because it makes life seem more "precious."

Well, as I said earlier in this chapter, Primo Levi was an Italian Jew who survived Auschwitz, and on page 146 of his book *The Drowned and the Saved*, he wrote that even though he wasn't religious himself, he noticed that religious prisoners were more likely than the average prisoner to survive, because their faith kept them from falling into despair. Apparently, instead of making life seem more "precious," the belief that death ends life absolutely just makes people feel depressed. But Dawkins never considers that possibility.

Dawkins also never worries that the belief that death ends everything might make people ignore their responsibilities and live only for immediate pleasure. On page 306 (page 346 of the paperback) Dawkins himself admits that religion makes people brave. If death ends everything, that means that the coward who dodged the draft during World War Two was smarter than the patriotic guy who went off to fight Hitler and got killed. Apparently Dawkins never thinks of that.

Look at Richard Feynman, a Nobel Prize-winning physicist who was not the least bit religious. (Endnote 131.) On page 132 of his memoir, *Surely You're Joking, Mr. Feynman*, Feynman says the famous mathematician John von Neumann persuaded him that he didn't need to care about justice, or about making the world a better place. "So I have developed a very powerful sense of social irresponsibility as a result of Von (sic) Neumann's advice," he writes. "It's made me a very happy man ever since."

All that atheist Feynman cared about was pleasure. But it never occurs to Dawkins that someone might think the way Feynman thought.

Look at the fact that Hamas won the Palestinian elections of 2007 because the religious fanatics of Hamas were much more honest than the less-religious politicians, much less prone to steal from the treasury and extort bribes from the common people. (Endnote 132.) The less-religious politicians are thinking that you only live once, so you must make as much money as possible as fast as possible in order to have as much pleasure as possible. But Dawkins never thinks of that either.

Look at corruption in politics in general. Why do so many politicians take bribes? Because they want to have fun right now. They think death ends everything and they do not fear Hell.

Look at any biography of Carl Sagan and you will see that he divorced his second wife when their son was only six years old, because he had met another woman whom he liked better, so he wanted to marry her. Surely Sagan visited his son from time to time in the following years, but there is simply no substitute for being right there in the home with the kid seven days a week, if you care about him. But what Sagan cared about was having fun right now. I wonder if he told his second wife, before he married her, "Oh, by the way, even after we get married, if I meet some woman I like better than you, I'll dump you and marry her." Somehow I doubt he was honest enough to tell her that.

That may sound like I'm joking, but I'm not. If you are the kind of person, like Sagan, who is going to dump your spouse, just because you've met someone you like better, then you have a moral duty to tell your spouse before you marry him or her that you are that kind of person. Divorcing your spouse when you've tried to make the marriage work, but you've drifted apart and the two of you agree about nothing and are constantly bickering, is one thing, but divorcing your spouse just because you've met someone you like better is something else, and any biography of Sagan will tell you that that is what he did. His second marriage was going along just fine. He had no significant complaints, and his second wife didn't want a divorce. But he met a woman he liked better than his second wife, so he traded in his second wife like a guy trading in an old car.

Item 112: Dawkins Lies About Pope Pius XII

On page 277 of *The God Delusion*, (page 314 of the paperback) Dawkins complains that Pope Pius XII refused to "take a stand against the Nazis."

Dawkins is lying. For proof of that, see a book I wrote called *Pope Pius XII – Not Guilty!* Here's a brief summary of the evidence. In 1930, the Vatican's official newspaper declared in a front-page editorial that a Catholic could not belong to the Nazi Party. (Endnote 133.) In 1937, Pope Pius XI issued a pastoral letter to the German people called *Mit Brennender Sorge* in which he denounced Nazism. (Endnote 134.) When Pius XII became pope, he never retracted either one of those statements. In January 1940, the Vatican radio station broadcasted a report that accused the Nazis of committing atrocities in Poland. (Endnote 135.) Later that same year, when Hitler invaded Belgium, the Netherlands and Luxemburg, Pius XII sent telegrams of support to the monarchs of those countries and had the texts of those telegrams published in the Vatican's official newspaper. (Endnote 136.) In December 1942, Pius XII delivered a speech over the Vatican radio station in which he lamented that there were in Europe "hundreds of thousands of persons who, without any fault on their part, sometimes only because of their nationality or race, have been consigned to death or to a slow decline." (Endnote 137.) In July 1943, the Vatican radio station broadcast Archbishop Stepinac's denunciation of anti-Jewish legislation. No government, Stepinac said, "has the right to persecute a man because of his race." (Endnote 138.) When some German generals who were plotting to overthrow Hitler sent an envoy to Pius XII, asking him to help them by delivering a message to the British, Pius did it. (Endnote 139.)

And look at Sweden. The socialist government there spent the war selling iron ore to Hitler, so he could manufacture his rifles, tanks and airplanes. Hitler got 40 percent of his iron from Sweden. (Endnote 140.) If Hitler had gotten 40 percent of his iron from the pope, can you imagine how Dawkins would yell about that? But apparently Dawkins isn't willing to criticize socialists.

Item 113: Dawkins Has Faith in David Mills

On page 44 of *The God Delusion*, (page 66 of the paperback) Dawkins tells us the saga of David Mills. Mills claims that when a faith healer came to his hometown for a revival meeting, he, Mills, wanted to demonstrate against the faith healer outside the meeting hall, but he asked "seven or eight" police officers if they would protect him from violence if he did that, and none said they would, and some threatened him.

If this story is true, why doesn't Dawkins tell us the name of the town, the name of the faith-healer, the names of the police officers, and the name of the police chief? That is what any good journalist would do. If somebody is doing something rotten, and you want to put a stop to it, you have to name names.

Furthermore, why does Mills think the police have an obligation to be his personal bodyguards every time he feels like protesting something? I would never expect the police to do that for me. Does Mills really think the police have nothing better to do? Wouldn't it be better for the police to spend their time patrolling in high-crime neighborhoods, or hanging around the parking lots of taverns to see if anyone tries to drive drunk?

And why does Dawkins believe Mills's story? He never explains that. Does he simply believe, on faith, every person who has a complaint about the police? If he does, he'll end up believing quite a few crackpots. Has Dawkins never heard of Tawana Brawley, a teenage girl in New York City who created a big stir years ago by falsely claiming some police officers kidnapped her and sexually assaulted her? If he hasn't, he can go to the Proquest Newspaper Database and look her up in the *New York Times*.

Cases of people falsely claiming to be the victims of hate crimes are more common than one might think. Donald Altschiller, the author of *Hate Crimes: A Reference Handbook*, has recorded almost two hundred such incidents in the last twenty-five years. (Endnote 141.) At Vassar College in 2013, a transgender student named Genesis Hernandez wrote anti-transgender graffiti on the walls in some dormitories, then filed a report to complain about it. In 2012, a lesbian college student named Alexandra Pennell claimed someone had slipped anti-lesbian hate letters into her dorm room, under the door. An investigation using a hidden camera eventually discovered that Pennell herself was the one who was doing it. In 2011, a black law student in Virginia claimed he had been racially profiled and harassed by university police. That was proven false. Perhaps the most bizarre incident occurred in 2004, when a psychology professor at Claremont McKenna vandalized her own car, claimed she was the victim of a hate crime, and tried to collect the insurance money. Would Dawkins be surprised to hear that people do such things?

One can name a number of other famous cases of people peddling phony stories. Three journalists named Michael Finkel, Jayson Blair and Stephen Glass became famous because of the lies they told. (Endnote 142.)

In 1972, a chap named Clifford Irving wrote a biography of Howard Hughes, and claimed to have gotten inside information by interviewing Hughes himself. This turned out to be false. (Endnote 143.)

A journalist named Alex Heard wrote an article in the March 19, 2007 issue of *New Republic* magazine, in which he proved beyond all doubt that the famous writer David Sedaris has lied in his nonfiction books.

A chap named James Frey wrote a memoir that sold two million copies and won the enthusiastic praise of Oprah Winfrey, but some of the incidents described in the book turned out to be phony. (Endnote 144.) Boy, was Oprah angry when she found out.

Joseph Mitchell, one of the most famous American journalists of the twentieth century, sometimes lied in his articles. He himself admitted that he felt no need to be "over-precise" or "over-documentary." That, of course, is just a fancy way of saying he didn't care about honesty. (Endnote 145.)

Brian Williams, a prominent TV journalist, got into a peck of trouble because it was proven that he had lied on the air about being in a helicopter that was hit by enemy fire, and lied on the air about some experiences he had during Hurricane Katrina. (Endnote 146.)

Gloria Steinem, the famous feminist, recently admitted that she lied on exams when she was in college. "I'd make up a great quote and attribute it to an important thinker," she said. "The professor would be impressed." (Endnote 147.) It is amazing that Steinem doesn't seem to realize that this is something she should be ashamed of.

On page 82 of the January/February 2016 issue of *Discover* magazine, we can read about Dong-Pyou Han, a medical researcher at Iowa State University, who was convicted in 2015 of fraud and sentenced to 57 months in prison. He falsified test results to make it look like an HIV vaccine was working better than it really was.

A lady named Shere Hite became famous in the 1980s for writing pop psychology books. When her survey methods were criticized, she went on Oprah Winfrey's television show and claimed Herbert Gans, the president of the American Sociological Association, had said her survey methods were "great." That was a lie. Gans had said no such thing. (Endnote 148.)

In 2005, a scientist named Hwang Woo-suk claimed to have made a major discovery in the field of biochemistry. Alas, the claim turned out to be false. (Endnote 149.)

A chap named Michael A. Bellesiles won the Bancroft Prize in 2001 for a book he had written about the history of gun ownership in the United States. Eventually the prize was rescinded because proof emerged that he had lied repeatedly in the book. (Endnote 150.)

A Dutch psychology professor named Diederik Stapel published dozens of studies in major journals for years, based on falsified data. (Endnote 151.)

Dawkins's friend Steven Pinker tells an interesting story on pages 318-319 of his book, *The Better Angels of Our Nature: Why Violence Has Declined*. The *Lancet*, a prestigious British medical journal, published an article in 2006 that estimated that 655,000 Iraqis had died because of George W. Bush's invasion of Iraq and its aftermath. In contrast, the World Health Organization said no, only about 110,000 deaths occurred because of the invasion and its aftermath. Pinker says he believes the World Health Organization, and thinks the *Lancet* study was severely flawed. One has to wonder if the people who did the *Lancet* study were motivated by bias, conscious or unconscious, against Bush.

William Faulkner, the famous novelist, went to Canada during World War One and joined the British air force. The war ended while he was still in training, so he was sent home without ever seeing combat, yet when he got home to Mississippi, he claimed he had been wounded in action and had a surgical steel plate in his head. (Endnote 152.)

There is ample reason to believe that Ernest Hemingway greatly exaggerated his heroism in World War One. (Endnote 153.)

When running for vice president in 1920, Franklin Roosevelt lied by claiming he had written the constitution of Haiti. (Endnote 154.)

A man who called himself Binjamin Wilkomirski wrote a book years ago about his experiences as an inmate in Auschwitz. It got rave reviews, but it turned out to be as phony as a 3-dollar bill. Wilkomirski's real name was Bruno Grosjean, he wasn't Jewish, he was never anywhere near Auschwitz during the Holocaust, and he was never imprisoned by the Nazis anywhere else either. (Endnote 155.)

Daniel Ortega, the president of Nicaragua, and a hero to many American leftists in the 1980s, has been accused of rape. His stepdaughter says she was raped by him several times when she was a teenager. He denies it. (Endnote 156.) Obviously, one of them is lying.

A prominent gay rights activist named Larry Kramer claimed in 1999 to have found an old diary that proved Abraham Lincoln was gay. Historians pronounced his evidence ridiculous. (Endnote 157.) It is just about certain that Kramer knew his evidence was phony. He would have have to have been a total idiot not to.

I could, of course, give many other examples. Doesn't Dawkins know that people lie a lot? So why does Dawkins believe David Mills? In any event, I'm not going to believe Mills's tale of woe when there is no evidence to back it up except his uncorroborated say-so. Mills himself seems to be a bit of an oddball. He was interviewed for an article in the December 13, 2015 issue of a British newspaper called *The Observer*, and said he "doesn't really like to be around people." He also said he is trying to invent robots that will be very much like women, so men will buy them in order to have sex with them.

It reminds me of a skit from *Saturday Night Live* in the 1970s where Steve Martin played a goofy guy in bib overalls who went on a TV talk show and claimed he had had sex with Margaret Trudeau, the first lady of Canada at the time. Would Dawkins believe a guy like that too?

Item 114: More Atheist Terrorism

On page 389 of *The God Delusion*, (page 437 of the paperback) Dawkins claims a man named Larry Hooper was murdered for being an atheist. What he doesn't mention is that the killer, a guy named Arthur Shelton, was mentally ill. Shelton and Hooper were roommates, and Shelton thought Hooper was a demon. You can see this by going to the website of the U.S. Court of Appeals for the Sixth Circuit and looking up case number 14-2093.

As I said earlier, Timothy McVeigh was a self-proclaimed agnostic, and he killed 168 people in the Oklahoma City bombing, but Dawkins says nothing about McVeigh. That doesn't interest him. Instead he talks about this one pathetic mental patient, Arthur Shelton.

Item 115: The NEW YORK TIMES

Dawkins complains on and on about discrimination against atheists, but the *New York Times Book Review* used to have a policy of excluding religious books from its bestseller lists. (Endnote 158.) *The Seven Storey Mountain* by Thomas Merton, though it sold very well, never appeared on the *New York Times* bestseller list, never received the free publicity that books get when they appear on that list, simply because it was the autobiography of a Catholic monk. If the United States is dominated by Christianity, the way Dawkins claims it is, why did that happen?

Item 116: Personhood

Dawkins wrote an essay years ago for a book called *This Idea Must Die*, edited by John Brockman, in which he rants about how stupid he thinks the anti-abortion movement is, because, he says, fetal development is so gradual that there is no point at which one can say the fetus has achieved "personhood." He also says that because humans are related to all other animals on Earth, abortion shouldn't be considered murder unless killing a chimp is considered murder too.

Once again, Dawkins is not being logical. He can't seem to understand that we have to have laws. We can't legalize everything. What exactly does he want the legal system to do? He never makes that clear. He never says that he wants abortion to be legal up to this point or that point. Doesn't he understand that all his talk is meaningless unless he does that? One almost gets the impression that he wants abortion to be legal on demand for all nine months of pregnancy, but he doesn't say that, and I find it hard to believe that he could seriously believe that, because even Hillary Clinton doesn't believe that. So where do you draw the line, Mr. Dawkins? Unless we are going to have abortion legal for all nine months, we have to draw the line somewhere.

Obviously, most people in the pro-life movement think we should draw the line at zero, that human life begins at conceptions, that abortion is always the killing of a human being. And contrary to Dawkins, they think that is more serious than the killing of a chimp.

Item 117: Aliens from Outer Space

In Chapter 1 of his book *The Selfish Gene*, in the very first paragraph, Dawkins writes "If superior creatures from space ever visit earth, the first question they will ask, in order to assess the level of our civilization, is 'Have they discovered evolution yet?'"

One feels astonished to read such stuff. Isn't it possible that the aliens would care, first and foremost, about morality? Isn't it possible that they would care about human rights and the rule of law and charity for the needy? Dawkins never thinks of that. Apparently he cares so little about such matters that it never occurs to him that aliens might be interested in them.

Even if one thinks the aliens would care about science above all, why would anyone assume they would inquire about evolution rather than about genetic engineering, relativity, quantum mechanics or nuclear power? Dawkins never explains that, because he can't. He has no explanation. All he has is an obsession with evolution that makes it impossible for him to see that most people are not as interested in it as he is. Tell us, Mr. Dawkins, what makes you so doggone sure the aliens wouldn't ask if we've discovered quantum mechanics? What makes you so doggone sure they wouldn't ask if we've discovered black holes, or cured cancer?

Item 118: Dawkins Complains About Humanities Professors

In the second paragraph of Chapter 1 of his book, *The Selfish Gene*, Dawkins writes, "Philosophy and the subjects known as 'humanities' are still taught almost as if Darwin had never lived. No doubt this will change in time."

What on Earth is Dawkins talking about? Why in the world would one teach differently about Shakespeare, Faulkner, Kant, Mozart, Michelangelo and Rembrandt just because of Darwin's theory? I can see no reason why one would do that, and Dawkins never explains why he thinks that will happen.

Item 119: The Moral Justification for War

In the March 17, 2004 issue of the *Independent*, a prominent British newspaper, there is a debate between Dawkins and someone named Johann Hari about George W. Bush's invasion of Iraq. Hari argues that when a cruel dictator is committing mass murder against his own people, it is good for other countries to invade his country and overthrow him. Dawkins replies that he has "great sympathy" for that idea, but he nevertheless opposes it because he thinks it sets a "dangerous precedent."

So there we have it. If Hitler had never invaded a foreign country, if he had merely butchered millions of people inside Germany, Dawkins would've shrugged and said "Let him do it." He writes, "It is a dangerous precedent that a country unilaterally invades any other country whose internal policies it happens to dislike. Many governments in the world disapprove of at least one of their neighbors. What if India invoked the precedent to invade Pakistan? Or North Korea to invade South Korea?"

It is obvious what would happen if India invaded Pakistan. The United Nations would condemn India for doing it and impose economic sanctions, and perhaps even authorize its members to take military action to defend Pakistan. The same is true about North Korea invading South Korea.

Let me make this clear: when Dawkins worries about precedent, he is being silly. Anyone who has studied history knows that precedent counts for nothing in international relations. Does Dawkins seriously believe that some dictator is going to think the world will let him get away with invading some other country, just because the world did nothing to stop George W. Bush from invading Iraq? Surely no dictator on Earth is foolish enough to think that way. Any dictator who wants to invade some other country is going to think only about whether the world will let him get away with it in this particular case, and anyone can see that this will depend entirely on the details of that particular case, not on any so-called precedent from the past. For example, Argentina invaded the Falkland Islands in 1982, not because of any precedent, but simply because Argentina's top generals and admirals thought the British were too lazy and/or cowardly to go to war over such a small piece of land with so few people on it. For another example, when Saddam Hussein invaded Iran in 1980, he did it because he saw that hardly anybody on Earth was friendly toward the Iranian government, and therefore he believed nobody would punish him for invading Iran. And he was right about that. To mention another example, when Vladimir Putin invaded Ukraine, he did it because he knew neither the United States nor anybody else on Earth cared enough about Ukraine to go to war for it, especially considering that Russia had a large arsenal of nuclear weapons. Precedent had nothing to do with it.

I think it is significant here that the two examples Dawkins uses, of India invading Pakistan or North Korea invading South Korea, are both totally out of the question. The Indians won't invade Pakistan as long as Pakistan has nuclear bombs, and the North Koreans won't invade South Korea because they know they could not possibly win that war, because the Americans would rush to South Korea's aid. Why doesn't Dawkins come up with a realistic scenario? Because there isn't one. There is simply no realistic scenario in which some government on this Earth might think it will get away with aggression because of the precedent of George W. Bush invading Iraq in 2003. Why can't Dawkins admit that?

Some people may think Dawkins couldn't possibly have been serious when he said he wouldn't have invaded Nazi Germany to stop mass murder. Some people may think he must've just expressed himself rather clumsily. I'm afraid that is not a possibility, because a few months later, in the October 13, 2004 issue of the *Guardian*, another British newspaper, Dawkins declared once again that one should never invade a foreign country just because it is ruled by a cruel dictator who is committing mass murder. He admits that "the world is a better place" now that Saddam Hussein has been ousted from power, but says George W. Bush, Tony Blair and their allies still shouldn't have invaded Iraq, because "It's not how civilized countries, who follow the rule of law, behave." He said this was his main reason for hoping that John Kerry would defeat George W. Bush in the 2004 presidential election.

People are being slaughtered, and Dawkins sits there babbling that we can't do anything about it because of international law. Is he out of his mind? I can understand a person in 2003 might have opposed the invasion of Iraq on the grounds that the invasion would surely cause Iraq to collapse into chaos, with horrendous loss of life. That would've been a reasonable argument back in 2003, and in fact, it turned out to be more or less accurate. I can also understand someone who says we shouldn't send troops to every country on Earth that is having serious problems, because we can't afford to do that. War is expensive, and we Americans would bankrupt ourselves if we tried to put an end to all injustice everywhere. But to oppose the invasion simply because one thinks it sets a bad precedent, when the obvious truth is that it sets no precedent at all, is like mistaking shadows for substance.

Item 120: Christopher Hitchens

In the British newspaper, the *Guardian*, on December 13, 2010, Dawkins declared that the late atheist journalist Christopher Hitchens was "honest."

Maybe next Dawkins will tell us John F. Kennedy was monogamous.

You can read about Hitchens in my book *Christopher Hitchens Lied Like a Rug*. The man had no integrity whatever. One wonders if Dawkins is really so ignorant that he doesn't know that.

Item 121: Child Molesting

By this time, some readers may be wondering what Dawkins said about the Catholic Church's child molestation scandal. Well, in *The God Delusion*, he barely talks about it. On page 316 of the hardcover and page 355 of the paperback, he mentions it, but also mentions that during his boyhood he attended three boarding schools, and all three had employees who were known pedophiles, and nobody did anything about it.

When Dawkins reached adulthood, did he go to the police and inform them about the pedophiles at the boarding schools he attended? Apparently not. He certainly doesn't mention doing so. Apparently, just like the Catholic bishops, and like just about everyone else, he turned a blind eye to it. It reminds me of how, when I was growing up, children never wore bicycle helmets. They should have, obviously, but they just didn't. It was not the custom. Parents in those days who insisted that their children wear bicycle helmets would have been considered weird.

Anyone who pays attention to local news knows that it is fairly common for schoolteachers to be arrested for having sex with their students. The Boy Scouts and Big Brothers Big Sisters have had problems with child molestation. (In fact, according a report on page 9 of the November 27, 2020 issue of *The Week* magazine, more than 92,000 men in the United States have claimed they were sexually molested by Boy Scout officials. In contrast, only 10,667 people in the United States have made allegations of sexual misconduct against Catholic priests, according to an article by Laurie Goodstein in the February 27, 2004 *New York Times*.) We've all heard about the Penn State football team's scandal. Even the Oprah Winfrey Leadership Academy for Girls had to fire a high-ranking employee a few years ago for sexually molesting students. (Endnote 159.) A few years ago USA Swimming, the governing body for competitive swimming in the United States, ran into a scandal similar to the Catholic Church's scandal, with officials allegedly covering up for coaches who were sexually preying on minors. (Endnote 160.) A swimmer named Kelly Currin says her coach, Rick Curl, raped her several times, starting when she was just 13 years old. She is now suing USA Swimming over this, because she says she complained to the top people in USA Swimming about Curl, but they continued to let him coach. According to the *New York Times*, USA Swimming has been hit with at least eight such lawsuits in recent years. (Endnote 161.)

Ms. magazine also reported on the scandal in USA Swimming in an article by Michele Kort in the Fall 2014 issue. In 2014, a man named Chuck Wielgus, who was the executive director of USA Swimming for many years, was nominated for the International Swimming Hall of Fame. Nineteen women signed a petition opposing the nomination, saying they were raped by their swim coaches while Wielgus had a policy of ignoring rape accusations. Eventually Wielgus withdrew his nomination.

Then a similar scandal erupted in USA Gymnastics. The story was the same: girls and their parents complained to the top officials about the behavior of coaches and a team doctor, but the top officials shrugged and did nothing. (Endnote 162.)

The world of Canadian hockey has also been rocked by sex abuse scandals. In 1997, a very successful junior hockey league coach named Graham James was convicted of hundreds of rapes committed against his teenaged players. After the death of Brian Shaw, the former chairman of the Western Hockey League board of governors, several people came forward and said he raped them when they were minors. (Endnote 163.)

Some of the most prestigious private secondary schools in the United States have had scandals similar to the Catholic Church's, and covered them up just like the Catholic bishops did. *New Yorker* magazine had an article in the April 1, 2013 issue by a journalist named

Marc Fisher about child molestation scandals that have come to light in some of America's most prominent private high schools, such as Andover and Exeter. The article concentrates on the Horace Mann school in New York City. Eighteen teachers there have been accused of sexually abusing "more than thirty-five students over four decades." For years, the head masters and the board of trustees refused to take allegations of abuse seriously. Stephen Fife, one of the victims, says that when he complained to an administrator that he had been raped, the administrator just told him he couldn't prove it, and making a fuss about it would "impair his efforts to get into a good college." There was an especially large number of complaints about a teacher named Robert Berman, but none of the high-ranking people at Horace Mann picked up the phone, called the police and said, "Five different boys have accused Berman of rape in the last five years. Maybe you ought to investigate this guy." They didn't want bad publicity.

An alumnus of Horace Mann named Amos Kamil wrote an article about the place in the June 10, 2012 issue of the *New York Times Magazine*, in which he discussed at length a pedophile teacher named Johannes Somary. Kamil interviewed other teachers and found that they strongly suspected that Somary was raping students, but they did nothing. They were afraid of being fired if they rocked the boat, and afraid of damaging the reputation of the school. (How similar to the attitudes of the Catholic bishops.) Finally, Kamil interviewed Phil Foote, the fellow who was "head of school" at the time, and asked him why he didn't call the police about Somary. Foote responded with vague gibberish. The gist of his answer seems to be that in those days (the late 1970s and early 1980s) doing that was just unthinkable.

Kamil mentions two other teachers who were fired for sexual misconduct with students, but in those cases too, nobody called the police. The idea seemed to be that just firing them, and letting them move on to other schools, was punishment enough.

Another prestigious private school in New York City, the Poly Prep Country Day School, ignored complaints of sexual abuse by the football coach, Philip Foglietta, for years. (Endnote 164.) School officials have now admitted that, though they forced Foglietta to retire in 1991, they did not publicly announce why he was retiring, and they did not call the police or anyone else in law enforcement and tell them about the evidence they had found. Foglietta died in 1998 without ever being arrested for his crimes. (Endnote 165.)

Recently, at least forty former students of the elite St. George's School in Middletown, Rhode Island, accused some former staff members and fellow students of rape. School officials had fired some of the staff members over the years, but never called the police and never warned the fired employees' subsequent employers. (Endnote 166.)

Choate Rosemary Hall, the high school from which John F. Kennedy graduated, recently admitted that at least twelve teachers who worked there over the years were child molesters. School officials never reported them to the police and in some cases, wrote letters of recommendation for them so they could find work elsewhere. (Endnote 167.)

In 2014, thirty-four people accused officials at Yeshiva University in New York of covering up "hundreds of acts of abuse" against minors by university staff in the 1960s, 1970s, and 1980s. (Endnote 168.)

If there was a large atheist organization that worked with children, I'm sure it would be infiltrated by pedophiles too.

In Great Britain, the Labour Party is the largest left-wing party, and in 2017, a young lady named Bex Bailey said that back in 2011 a "more senior party member" raped her at a "party event." When she told a "senior member of staff" what happened, the only response she got was that she should keep silent because complaining might damage her career. (Endnote 169.) The Labour Party's leader, Jeremy Corbyn, admitted that the party needed to start making sure that perpetrators would not feel they could get away with such crimes.

Oxfam and Save the Children, two of the most respected charities in the English-speaking world, were recently found to have covered up cases of child molestation and sexual harassment by employees. (Endnote 170.) Why? Because making the truth public would have surely caused a drop in donations. And that is what the Catholic bishops were worried about too.

Item 122: William Lane Craig

There is a theology professor named William Lane Craig who has a reputation for being a very good debater. Dawkins frequently debates Christians, but in 2011 he was challenged to debate Craig and refused. Instead he posted a rant against Craig on the Internet, calling him "unctuous." One has to suspect he was simply afraid that he would lose a debate with Craig. (Endnote 171.) In addition to being a liar, Dawkins is also a coward.

Item 123: A Pretty Good Joke

On the plus side, Dawkins has provoked a pretty good joke. He likes telling atheist audiences that they should start calling themselves, "the brights." A journalist named David Stubbs quipped, "You might as well call yourself the smugs." (Endnote 172.)

Item 124: Dawkins Does Battle with Rebecca Watson

A few years ago, a militant atheist named Rebecca Watson attended some sort of atheist/skeptic convention in Ireland and spent the evening discussing various topics with the other attendees. At 4 a.m., she got into an elevator to go back to her hotel room and go to sleep. One of the men she had been talking to got on the elevator with her, and invited her to his room for coffee. She declined. Later she made a video about what she had seen at the convention, and posted it on Youtube, and among other things, she mentioned that being propositioned at 4 a.m. in an elevator, when she and the propositioner were the only people in the elevator, made her feel uncomfortable. She advised men to not do that. She did not make a big deal out of it, but for some reason, our buddy Dawkins took umbrage. He posted a sarcastic comment on a different website, calling the incident trivial and telling Watson she should just be glad she doesn't live in a Muslim country where she might have to suffer female circumcision. An Internet uproar ensued, with many people adding their comments. Feminists accused Dawkins of failing to imagine what it is like for women to constantly be pestered by sexually aggressive men, and Dawkins continued to insist that the man in the elevator had done nothing even slightly wrong. The incident became known as Elevatorgate, and you can read all about it by doing an Internet search for: rebecca watson dawkins elevatorgate.

I would be willing to bet that Watson and Dawkins agree about almost everything. Why couldn't Dawkins just shrug off a small disagreement? Apparently Dawkins is the kind of man who thinks the appropriate way to handle even the smallest disagreement is to fire a volley of insults and sarcasm. Maybe that explains why he has been divorced twice.

Item 125: Dawkins Angers the Feminists

Then in 2016, Dawkins ran into more trouble with women. You can read about it on the Internet. He sent out a tweet urging people to watch a video called *Feminists Love Islamists*. It was supposed to be funny, but actually, it was insulting, and about as funny as watching paint dry. Feminists were offended.

CONCLUSION

I think it is obvious that after the rather surprising commercial success of Sam Harris's book *The End of Faith*, Dawkins simply decided he could make big money by writing a book full of the kind of lies that atheists want to hear. Honesty means nothing to him. Perhaps now his colleagues are starting to see that. A recent survey of scientists found that many of them think Dawkins "misrepresents science." (Endnote 173.)

ENDNOTES

1. See the articles about Toland in the *New York Times* on January 7, 2004 and April 18, 2004, and in the *Los Angeles Times* on January 6, 2004.

2. See page 156 of *20th Century Journey: The Nightmare Years: 1930-1940*, by the famous CBS News journalist William L. Shirer.

3. See page 55 of Saul Friedlander's book, *The Years of Extermination: Nazi Germany and the Jews, 1939-1945*, which won a Pulitzer Prize.

4. See page 202 of the book *Hitler's Pope* by John Cornwell.

5. See page 203 of Saul Friedlander's book, *The Years of Extermination: Nazi Germany and the Jews, 1939-1945*, which won a Pulitzer Prize.

6. See pages 132-134 of the book *The Powers That Be* by David Halberstam.

7. See page 269 of Ian Buruma's critically-acclaimed book, *The Wages of Guilt: Memories of War in Germany and Japan.*

8. See pages 124 and 169 of the book *The Catholic Church and Nazi Germany*, by the famous Jewish historian Guenter Lewy.

9. Ibid, page 124.

10. Ibid, pages 171-174.

11. See page 279 of *The Rise and Fall of the Third Reich* by William L. Shirer.

12. See page 124 of *The Catholic Church and Nazi Germany* by Guenter Lewy.

13. Ibid, pages 130-150.

14. Ibid, page 227.

15. Ibid, page 233.

16. See page 26 of Michael Phayer's book, *The Catholic Church and the Holocaust, 1930-1965.*

17. See pages 424-425 of *Hitler, 1936-1945: Nemesis*, by Ian Kershaw.

18. See page 154 of Steven Pinker's book *The Blank Slate*.

19. See page 707 of *The First American: The Life and Times of Benjamin Franklin*, by H.W. Brands.

20. Ibid, pages 677-678.

21. Ibid, page 658.

22. See page 9 of *American Gospel: God, the Founding Fathers, and the Making of a Nation*, by Jon Meacham, the former managing editor of *Newsweek*.

23. You can read that speech on page 354 of the book *John Brown: Abolitionist*, by David S. Reynolds.

24. See page 16 of the November 3, 2012, issue of the *Economist* magazine.

25. See pages 33-36 of *The End of Days: Fundamentalism and the Struggle for the Temple Mount* by Gershom Gorenberg.

26. See Cathy Young's article about Eric Pianka in the April 17, 2006 *Boston Globe*.

27. See page 429 of the book *The Collected Essays, Journalism and Letters of George Orwell: My Country Right or Left, 1940-1943*, edited by Sonia Orwell and Ian Angus.

28. See page 331 of Steven Pinker's book, *The Blank Slate: The Modern Denial of Human Nature*.

29. See page 622 of *Einstein: The Life and Times* by Ronald W. Clark.

30. See pages 206-207 of Ronald W. Clark's book, *The Survival of Charles Darwin: A Biography of a Man and an Idea*.

31. See page 318 of the book *Darwin's Sacred Cause*, by Adrian Desmond and James Moore.

32. See page 251 of Samantha Power's book, *"A Problem from Hell": America in the Age of Genocide*.

33. See page 210 of *Origins of a Catastrophe* by Warren Zimmermann.

34. See pages 192, 201, 330 and 410-411 of the book, *Hearts Grown Brutal: Sagas of Sarajevo*, by Roger Cohen, a journalist for *New York Times*, and see page 97 of the book, *Milosevic: Portrait of a Tyrant*, by Dusko Doder, a former reporter for the *Washington Post*, and Louise Branson, a former reporter for the *Sunday Times* of London.

35. See page 210 of *Origins of a Catastrophe* by Warren Zimmermann.

36. Ibid, page 138; and pages 193 and 350 of *Hearts Grown Brutal: Sagas of Sarajevo*, by Roger Cohen.

37. See page 138 and pages 156-157 of *Origins of a Catastrophe* by Warren Zimmermann.

38. Ibid, page 177.

39. See Thomas L. Friedman's column in the June 7, 1995 *New York Times*.

40. See page 673 of Philip Norman's book, *John Lennon: The Life*.

41. See pages 49-52 of a biography of Golda Meir called *Golda*, by a journalism professor named Elinor Burkett.

42. See page 776 of *John Lennon: The Life*, by Philip Norman.

43. See page 228 of Peter Doggett's book, *You Never Give Me Your Money: The Beatles After the Breakup*.

44. See page 790 of *John Lennon: The Life*, by Philip Norman.

45. See page 268 of the book *You Never Give Me Your Money: The Beatles After the Breakup* by Peter Doggett.

46. See pages 413-414 of Albrecht Folsing's biography of Einstein, and page 208 of Walter Isaacson's book, *Einstein: His Life and Universe*, and pages 183 and 186 of *Einstein: The Life and Times*, by Ronald W. Clark.

47. See page 208 of *Einstein: His Life and Universe*, by Walter Isaacson.

48. See page 402 of Albrecht Folsing's biography of Einstein.

49. Ibid, page 597.

50. Ibid.

51. Ibid, pages 616-617, and pages 360-364 of *Einstein: His Life and Universe*, by Walter Isaacson.

52. See page 375 of the book *Ireland's Holy Wars: The Struggle for a Nation's Soul, 1500-2000*, by Marcus Tanner.

53. See page 408 of the book, *Warlord: A Life of Winston Churchill at War, 1874-1945*, by Carlo D'Este.

54. See page 3 of the book *They Never Said It*, by two college professors named John George and Paul F. Boller, Jr., published by the Oxford University Press, one of the most prestigious publishing houses in the world.

55. See page 146 of the version of Primo Levi's book, *The Drowned and the Saved*, that was published by Summit Books in 1988.

56. See Roger Olson's article on this subject on pages 87-93 of *Christianity Today*, Sept. 6, 1999, and pages 36, and 172-173 of William J. Bouwsma's book, *John Calvin: A Sixteenth-Century Portrait*.

57. See pages 154-162 of the book, *Why Does the World Exist? An Existential Detective Story* by Jim Holt.

58. See page 460 of the book *The Life of Bertrand Russell* by Ronald W. Clark.

59. Ibid, page 457.

60. Ibid, page 245.

61. See pages 129 and 209 of Robin Lane Fox's book *The Unauthorized Version: Truth and Fiction in the Bible*.

62. You can find these statements on pages 227 and 378-379 of *The Collected Essays, Journalism and Letters of George Orwell: As I Please, 1943-1945*, edited by Sonia Orwell and Ian Angus.

63. See Steven Pinker's book *The Blank Slate: The Modern Denial of Human Nature*, pages 16-29, 56-58, 106-120, and Pinker's book *The Better Angels of Our Nature*, pages 43-46.

64. See pages 339-340, 344-354, 358-359 of Steven Pinker's book, *The Blank Slate: The Modern Denial of Human Nature*.

65. See the article by Ruth Marcus in the October 3, 1988, issue of the *Washington Post*.

66. See pages 394 and 410 of *20th Century Journey: The Nightmare Years: 1930-1940*, by William L. Shirer.

67. See pages 103-104 of *The Collected Essays, Journalism and Letters of George Orwell: My Country Right or Left, 1940-1943*, edited by Sonia Orwell and Ian Angus.

68. Ibid, page 141.

69. See pages 425 and 728 of *Conduct Unbecoming: Gays and Lesbians in the U.S. Military* by Randy Shilts.

70. See page 409 of the book *The Ancestor's Tale: A Pilgrimage to the Dawn of Evolution* by Richard Dawkins.

71. See page 338 of Sean Wilentz's book, *The Rise of American Democracy: Jefferson to Lincoln*.

72. See pages 203-204 of *Harriet Tubman: Imagining a Life*, by Beverly Lowry.

73. See page 708 of the book *Alexander Hamilton* by the famous historian Ron Chernow.

74. See pages 195-197 and 320 of *Undaunted Courage: Meriweather Lewis, Thomas Jefferson, and the Opening of the American West*, by Stephen E. Ambrose.

75. See page 192 of Ronald W. Clark's book, *Einstein: The Life and Times*.

76. See page 259 of the book *Coming Apart: The State of White America, 1960-2010*, by Charles Murray.

77. See the section written by Craig in the book, *Will the Real Jesus Please Stand Up?* by William Lane Craig and John Dominic Crossan.

78. See the article by Jake Halpern in the August 10 & 17, 2015 issue of *New Yorker* magazine.

79. See Neal B. Freeman's article in the October 19, 2015, issue of *National Review* magazine.

80. See page 45 of the January 16, 2017 issue of *New Yorker* magazine.

81. See pages 79 and 250 of the book *Those Angry Days: Roosevelt, Lindbergh, and America's Fight Over World War II, 1939-1941*, by Lynne Olson.

82. See the article by Richard B. Freeman in the July 20, 1986 *New York Times*.

83. See Shariff and Norenzayan's article "Mean Gods Make Good People" in the April 2011 issue of *The International Journal for the Psychology of Religion*.

84. See the article by Michael Wines in the August 23, 2016 *New York Times*.

85. See page 435 of *Mencken: A Life*, by Fred Hobson, published by the Johns Hopkins University Press.

86. See Steven Erlanger's article in the September 26, 1995 *New York Times*. After the fall of communism, the cathedral was re-built.

87. See page 431 of *H.G. Wells: A Biography*, by Norman and Jean Mackenzie.

88. See pages 241-242 of Edward O. Wilson's book, *The Social Conquest of Earth*.

89. See pages 245-247 of Steven Pinker's book *The Blank Slate: The Modern Denial of Human Nature*.

90. See the article by Laurie Goodstein in the April 7, 2006 *New York Times*.

91. See pages 308-309 of *Constantine's Sword: The Church and the Jews*, by James Carroll.

92. See the article by Avishai Margalit in the March 9, 2017, *New York Review of Books*.

93. See page 126 of *The Unauthorized Version: Truth and Fiction in the Bible*, by the famous historian Robin Lane Fox.

94. See page 1048 of *The Rise and Fall of the Third Reich* by William L. Shirer.

95. See page 33 of the May 23, 2016 issue of *New Yorker* magazine.

96. See pages 345-346 of a book called *Charles Darwin: The Power of Place*, by a history professor named Janet Browne.

97. The facts about the Polanski case come from an article in the September 30, 2009, *New York Times*, by Michael Cieply and Doreen Carvajal, and an editorial in the same issue.

98. See an editorial in the *Washington Post* on December 13, 2005.

99. See Thomas L. Friedman's column in the February 18, 2015 *New York Times*.

100. See page 457 of Rick Perlstein's critically-acclaimed book, *Nixonland: The Rise of a President and the Fracturing of America*.

101. Ibid, page 475.

102. See page 429 of the book *The Collected Essays, Journalism and Letters of George Orwell: My Country Right or Left, 1940-1943*, edited by Sonia Orwell and Ian Angus.

103. See Cathy Young's article about Pianka in the April 17, 2006 *Boston Globe*.

104. See page 95 of *Conduct Unbecoming: Gays and Lesbians in the U.S. Military*, by Randy Shilts.

105. See page 261 of *The Life of Bertrand Russell* by Ronald W. Clark.

106. See page 722 of *John Lennon: The Life*, by Philip Norman.

107. Ibid, page 503.

108. See page 88 of the Spring 2009 issue of the *Wilson Quarterly*.

109. See page 342 of *Pagans and Christians* by the famous historian Robin Lane Fox.

110. Ibid.

111. See an article by Joyce Chen in the *New York Daily News*, September 21, 2012.

112. See JoAnn Wypijewski's article in the September 1999 issue of *Harper's* magazine.

113. See the article by Leslie Tentler in the October 9, 2015 issue of *Commonweal* magazine.

114. See page 280 of *The Gay Revolution: The Story of the Struggle*, by Lillian Faderman.

115. See page 70 of Gershom Gorenberg's book *The End of Days*.

116. See the article by Connie Bruck in the January 20, 2014 *New Yorker* magazine.

117. See the article by Patrick Radden Keefe in the October 30, 2017 issue of *New Yorker* magazine.

118. See page 16 of the March 2009 issue of *Scientific American* magazine.

119. See Ian Johnston's article in the August 21, 2014 issue of the *Independent*, a British newspaper.

120. See pages 249-251 of Edward O. Wilson's book, *Consilience: The Unity of Knowledge*.

121. See an article by James Bennet in the March 29, 2002 *New York Times*, the article by Elaine Sciolino in the June 16, 2002 *New York Times*, and the article by Jim Hoagland in the November 24, 2002 *Washington Post*.

122. For the facts about this, see George Monbiot's article in the September 22, 2009 issue of the *Guardian* newspaper.

123. See an editorial on this subject called "Progress Where They Make iPhones" in the December 30, 2012 *New York Times*.

124. See pages 423-424 of of the book *Bully for Brontosaurus: Reflections in Natural History*, by the famous biology professor Stephen Jay Gould.

125. See an article about Matthew Murray in the December 11, 2007 *Denver Post*.

126. See articles about Craig Stephen Hicks in the *New York Times*, February 13, 2015 and March 4, 2015.

127. See the article by Julian Borger in the June 11, 2001 issue of the socialist British newspaper, the *Guardian*.

128. See an article by Jacey Fortin in the July 25, 2017 *New York Times*.

129. See pages 292 and 475-476 of *The Dark Side of Genius: The Life of Alfred Hitchcock*, by Donald Spoto.

130. See an article by Ian Fisher in the April 21, 2007 *New York Times*, and an article by Tracy Wilkinson in the April 21, 2007 *Los Angeles Times*.

131. See page 438 of *Genius: The Life and Science of Richard Feynman*, by James Gleick.

132. See the editorial "Eyeless in Gaza" in the July 9, 2007, issue of the *Nation* magazine.

133. See page 116 of John Cornwell's book *Hitler's Pope*.

134. Ibid, pages 181-184; or go to *The Rise and Fall of the Third Reich* by William L. Shirer, look up the pages that mention Pius XI in the index, and read those pages.

135. See page 28 of *Pius XII, the Holocaust and the Cold War* by Michael Phayer.

136. See pages 242-243 of *Hitler's Pope* by John Cornwell.

137. See page 53 of *Pius XII, the Holocaust and the Cold War* by Michael Phayer.

138. Ibid, page 13.

139. See page 239 of *Hitler's Pope* by John Cornwell.

140. See pages 83-84 of *Postwar: A History of Europe Since 1945*, by the famous historian Tony Judt.

141. See page 127 of the third edition of *Hate Crimes: A Reference Handbook* by Donald Altschiller.

142. See an article by Robert Darnton in the June 28, 2018 *New York Review of Books*.

Endnotes

143. See the article by Motoko Rich in the March 8, 2008 *New York Times*.

144. See the article by Edward Wyatt in the January 27, 2006 *New York Times*.

145. See Ruth Franklin's article about Joseph Mitchell in the June 2015 *Atlantic Monthly*.

146. See the article about Brian Williams in the February 14, 2015 *Washington Post*.

147. See the article about Steinem in the October 19, 2015 issue of *New Yorker* magazine.

148. See the article about Shere Hite in the November 13, 1987 *New York Times*.

149. See articles about Hwang Woo-suk in the *New York Times*: December 23, 24, and 29 in 2005.

150. See the articles about Bellesiles in the following issues of the *New York Times*: December 8, 2001, October 27, 2002, and December 14, 2002.

151. See Carey Benedict's article in the June 16, 2015 *New York Times*.

152. See pages 22-24 of the book, *William Faulkner: The Man and the Artist* by Stephen B. Oates.

153. See pages 82-86 of *Hemingway* by Kenneth S. Lynn.

154. See pages 230-231 of *FDR: A Biography* by Ted Morgan.

155. See the article by Walter Goodman in the December 29, 1999 *New York Times*.

156. See the article about Daniel Ortega in the June 19, 1998 *New York Times*.

157. See the article by Stephanie Simon in the June 22, 1999 *Los Angeles Times*.

158. See an article by Robert Giroux in the October 11, 1998 *New York Times Book Review*.

159. See the Wikipedia article about the Oprah Winfrey Leadership Academy for Girls.

160. See Karen Crouse's articles in the May 20, 2010, May 24, 2013, and June 19, 2013 issues of the *New York Times*.

161. Ibid.

162. See an article by Jennifer Sey in the April 2, 2017 *New York Times*.

163. See an article by Anthony DePalma in the January 16, 1997 *New York Times*.

164. See the article by Peter Schworm in the February 14, 2013 *Boston Globe*.

165. See the article by Sophia Hollander in the February 22, 2014 *Wall Street Journal*.

166. See the article by Katherine Seelye in the January 6, 2016 *New York Times*.

167. See the article by Elizabeth A. Harris in the April 14, 2017 *New York Times*.

168. See the article by Ariel Kaminer in the January 31, 2014 *New York Times*.

169. See the article by Rowena Mason and Anushka Asthana in the November 1, 2017 issue of the *Guardian* newspaper.

170. See Lizzie Dearden's article in the March 16, 2018 issue of the British newspaper, the *Independent*, and Sean O'Neill's articles in the March 8, 2016 and March 9, 2016 *Times* of London.

171. See the article about this in the October 23, 2011, issue of a British newspaper, the *Independent*.

172. See David Stubbs's article in the March 1, 2008, issue of the *Guardian* newspaper.

173. See page 28 of the November 14, 2016 issue of *New Yorker* magazine.

Other Books by the Same Author

Darwin Wanted to Exterminate the Blacks, and Other Facts About Famous Atheists

    Christopher Hitchens Lied Like a Rug

    Carl Sagan Lied Like a Rug

    Sam Harris Lies Like a Rug

    Enlightenment How? The Lies and Evasions of Steven Pinker

    Evolution Favors People Who Don't Believe in Evolution

    Let's Clone Abraham Lincoln

    Biochemistry Will Kill Us All

    Intelligence is Genetic

    Nicholas Kristof Doesn't Know What He Is Talking About

    Michelle Obama Doesn't Know What He is Talking About

    The Dinosaur Who Became Vice President: A Work of Science Fiction